The Black Virgin

A Marian Mystery

JEAN HANI

The Black Virgin

A Marian Mystery

ANGELICO PRESS
SOPHIA PERENNIS

Originally published in French as
La Vierge Noire et le mystère marial
© Guy Trédaniel, Éditions de la Maisnie, 1995
First published in USA
by Sophia Perennis © 2007
Angelico Press / Sophia Perennis edition © 2016

Translated by Robert Proctor
Edited by G. John Champoux and Marie Hansen
Series editor: James R. Wetmore

For information, address:
Angelico Press
4709 Briar Knoll Dr.
Kettering, OH 45429
angelicopress.com

Library of Congress Cataloging-in-Publication Data

Hani, Jean.
[Vierge noire et le mystère marial. English]
The black virgin: a marian mystery / Jean Hani.

p. cm.
ISBN 1 59731 064 2 (pbk: alk. paper)
1. Black Virgins. I. Title.
BT670.B55H3613 2006
246'.5—dc22   2006021558

Cover Design: Michael Schrauzer

CONTENTS

TO
THE BLESSED VIRGIN MARY,
MOTHER OF GOD AND MOTHER OF MEN

Introduction

THIS WORK does not fit into the category of the many books on the Black Virgins already published, and we shall immediately start by reviewing these in order to better define the purpose of our own. So as not to burden with constant citations, notes and references the reading of a book conceived as a doctrinal exposition rather than a work of scholarly research, we shall list just this once the principal titles used in our research, leaving aside works that only touch on the Black Virgins in passing, as well as those that deal only with a particular example.

First, let us mention a long-forgotten essay: Madame Durand-Lefevre's thesis, *Étude sur l'origine des Vierges noires*. As far as we know, this was the first combined historical and archeological work on the question of the Black Virgins. It continues to be of interest and also has the advantage of giving all of the earlier bibliography, often scattered in inaccessible publications or places. But, following after her, E. Saillens' *Nos Vierges noires* (Paris, 1938) really posed and dealt with the necessary questions, albeit still from an historical and archeological point of view. His work remains a model of scientific rigor in the choice, treatment and clear-sighted interpretation of documents. It is *the* reference book, and the more one reads it, the more one realizes that Saillens truly saw and posed all the problems —and we really mean *all* the problems—and it is amazing to see that he even outlined valuable solutions for problems outside of his own historico-critical area, such as alchemy.

There is also Sophie Cassagnes Brouquet's book, *Vierges noires, regard et fascination*, (Rodez, 1990) which adds nothing new. Although a scientifically reputable work, it is deliberately somewhat 'light' in the sense that it in no way attempts an exhaustive examination of the material and the problems raised; it is nevertheless a worthwhile and well-illustrated book of serious popularization.

1

The three authors just cited confine themselves to an essentially historical and archeological point of view. Others, who have clearly seen that the Black Virgins belong to a religious and spiritual current that cannot be satisfactorily explained using the analytical tools of the historico-critical method, have sought to elucidate the matter by appealing to traditional sciences such as sacred geography and alchemy. These include J. Huynens, in *L'Enigme des Vierges noires* (Paris, 1972; Brussels, 1984), J. Bovin, in *Vierges noires, la reponse vient de la terre* (Paris, 1988), and the collaborators in two special editions of the revue *Atlantis* dedicated to the Black Virgins (No: 205-206 (1961), to which we should add a long article by R. Marlière published in no.355 (1988). But, despite their brevity, we have given most attention to two fundamental articles of great value: Pierre Gordon's 'Les Vierges noires' republished in the volume *Essais* (Arma Artis, 1983) and Max Escalon de Fonton's 'La tradition des Vierges noires' (*Connaissance des religions* IV, 1–2 (1988). The latest work to appear, Roland Berman's *Vierges noires, Vierges initiatrices* (Paris, 1993) unfortunately came out too late for us to use, for at the time, although not yet published, our book was already all but finished.

The perspective of these last authors is not only legitimate but necessary. Once the historical foundations of the origin and development of the Black Virgins has been firmly established, the question of their meaning and role can only be answered by appealing to religious, and secondarily to traditional, sciences. In this sphere, also, it is necessary to be well-informed and to follow a rigorous method, but this is not always the case. Some of the authors just cited, while offering very interesting perspectives, do not possess a sufficient philosophical and especially theological background, and this leads them to commit enormous 'blunders' like, 'The message of Christ was not to replace the old dogmas but to reassemble them in a cosmic synarchy,' or, again, to show their total ignorance of liturgy and Patristic exegesis by writing that the *Song of Songs* 'is a non-prophetic poem . . . and does not have the slightest connection with the Holy Virgin'(sic)! However, their ignorance in these matters does not prevent them from passing some incisive and definitive judgments, nor, on occasion, from displaying their disdain and even hostility towards religion. This is not a good attitude for a profound understanding of spiritual things.

In fact, what for the most part has stimulated the interest of so many of our contemporaries in the phenomenon or 'enigma' (as one of the just cited authors puts it) of the Black Virgins, is above all the strange and unusual way in which they are depicted. Contemporary man, at least, finds the depictions 'strange' and 'enigmatic', but it was obviously not so for the Mediaeval Christian who knew exactly what he was dealing with. In addition, there is also an attractive element to these figures, the 'fascination' exercised by the better specimens, at least. Without a doubt, the black statues of the Virgin are among the most powerful forms of sacred art. No eastern icon of the Virgin contains an equal charge, or 'voltage' of the sacred. We have, moreover, a proof of this *a contrario*, in the extent and fury of the hatred and violence they suffered at the hands of subversive forces, whose instruments were the Huguenots in the sixteenth century, and the revolutionary mobs at the end of the eighteenth—two occasions when subversion was manifested spectacularly in an attempt to destroy every sign of the sacred. During the first period, the Reformation made religion into something sentimental and moralizing, a preamble to the establishment in the second of a veritable rationalist and scientistic counter-religion.

These black statues of Mary have been classified according to their most common size, posture, and the manner in which they look at the spectator, in an attempt to grasp their uniqueness, to explain the fascination and strange character that belongs to them, but all these supposedly characteristic traits also belong to all light-complexioned 'Virgins in Majesty'. And attempts to penetrate the secret of the figure in terms of site and surroundings, like the grotto, tree, and spring, etc., to deduce therefrom that close bonds exist between the Virgin thus represented and nature, ends in a similar dead end: the majority of Marian cult sites have these elements in common. We get no further, finally, when we seek to characterize the Black Virgin in terms of her influence on the fertility of the earth, animals, and humans, or miracles such as the liberation of besieged towns, the deliverance of prisoners, the rescue of the shipwrecked and the raising of the dead, for these are the same deeds with which the Virgin is

3

credited wherever she is venerated under the form of a 'white' statue. In fact, we are finally led to conclude that the only trait truly characteristic of the Black Virgin is... her blackness!

It is this, therefore, that needs to be explained.

To be sure, there is the well-established fact that these statues succeeded those of the pre-Christian mother-goddesses represented under the same color. But then the problem rebounds at two levels: why were these goddesses black in hue? And why was this color appropriate to Mary, so that it passed from them to her? In other words, the problem is clearly much wider, for it concerns the transition from the cult of the mother-goddesses to that of Mary, for in the veneration of the people, Mary was successor not only to the black goddesses, but to all the mother-goddesses found within the area of Christian expansion, the great majority of whom were 'white'.

It is thus no longer only an historical and archeological problem, but a theological one of unusual magnitude. In fact, it is a question of explaining how a form belonging to a *polytheistic* religion was able to pass into a strictly *monotheistic* religion like Christianity, so as to inspire a certain conception of the cult of the Virgin Mary.

It is easy to see that the explanation can only come from a study of the very nature of the Virgin, or, if one prefers, her ontological status and its possible correspondences, within the monotheistic perspective, with the divinities concerned.

Moreover, it is here that the principal gap in the majority of works dedicated to the Black Virgins manifests itself, the authors being extremely ill-informed concerning Marian science, be it theology, liturgy, or mystical writings, with the result that the final explanation of the problem eludes them. The only two authors who have seen the explanation clearly are P. Gordon and Max Escalon de Fonton, in the short articles cited above.

The task thus consists in explaining what religious tradition and theology call the 'Mystery of Mary' or the 'Marian Mystery'. For, even if there is no 'enigma' of the Black Virgins, to quote the title of a well-known book, there is a 'mystery of the Black Virgin', which is ultimately, however, none other than the total Marian Mystery, or, to be still more precise, a certain *aspect* of the Mystery, or again, this Mystery seen from a particular perspective.

Does this mean that this particular aspect is only of secondary importance? Certainly not; besides, why in that case would we undertake the present study? On the contrary, we shall see that the meaning of the Black Virgin, illumined by the total Marian Mystery, permits in return the plumbing of this Mystery in itself—this is important—as it applies to the practice of the Marian cult in the service of human life.

When we speak of 'mystery', what exactly do we mean by the term? We understand it in the official religious sense of the more or less symbolic expression of a transcendent reality that surpasses the ordinary rational mode of thought. The object of the mystery is not, however, the irrational but the supra-rational; it is not, as is popularly thought, 'what one does not understand,' but, according to the definition of St Augustine, 'what, aided by Divine Grace, one has never finished understanding,' given that it opens the spirit to ineffable and inexhaustible realities.

The content of the mystery pertains to revealed data confided to the Magisterium of the Church, which has the duty to explain it according to the needs of the faithful. Thus Revelation and its mysteries develop in response to the variations in human perspectives over time. Consequently, there is a progression in the understanding of the object of any particular mystery. This development is particularly striking in the case of the Marian mystery. The Gospels say very little about the earthly career of the Virgin, and limit themselves to reporting the essential events which have to do with Christ's own career: the Annunciation, the Nativity, the Presentation in the Temple, Cana, and Calvary. So too the writings of the Apostles. The oral tradition, however, and the reflections of the Fathers and theologians of the very first centuries led to the great revelation of the year 431 at the Council of Ephesus, proclaiming Mary *Theotokos*, that is to say 'Mother of God'.

This proclamation contains the *whole* Marian Mystery, but in a formula of such plenitude that its true import would only gradually come to be seen. Indeed, the culminating point was the event of March 25, 1858 at Lourdes, where the Virgin Mary proclaimed herself the 'Immaculate Conception'. This announcement is the most extraordinary celestial revelation accorded to humanity for a long time, and we have yet to completely fathom its profundity; let us rather say that both then and now very few have had any idea of the profundity of the dogma, even within the hierarchy of the Church, which had proclaimed the dogma only shortly before. Now, as we shall endeavor to show, this announcement is the key to the Marian Mystery in its transcendent dimension. And we shall then see, by way of consequence, that this key also furnishes us with the final explanation of what the Black Virgin represents.

Moreover, it will be most instructive to compare the revelation at Lourdes and the appearance, or reappearance, of numerous black images during the high point of Western Christianity, the eleventh and twelfth centuries. In our opinion, the relationship that exists between the appearance of the Black Virgins and the apparition at Lourdes is that of the close tie linking symbol to reality: the Black Virgin is the revelation to the Middle Ages, in symbolic mode, of the transcendent reality of the Mystery of Mary, revealed at Lourdes in direct mode.

Having thus clearly defined our intention, we shall in the first chapter, list the essential findings of the historical and archeological approach to the black images that today are considered most reliable, and which just now led us to raise the question of the transition from the cult of the pre-Christian mother-goddesses to that of the Virgin, and the practical assimilation of the former to the latter.

In order to determine the legitimacy of this assimilation, a legitimacy that in the final analysis can only be based on an authentically orthodox Christian foundation, we have thought it necessary first of all to examine as thoroughly as possible the identifiable common traits between the Virgin and the pre-Christian entities, and to see which can be reconciled with the theology, liturgy, authentic mysticism, and common, unchanging piety of Christianity. This is the aim of our second chapter, at the end of which, after the common traits have been authenticated by comparative analysis, we shall formulate the problem of the transition of a form pertaining to polytheism to a form, considered analogous in nature, pertaining to monotheism, that is, by asking the incisive question: should we, and can we, consider the Virgin to be divine?

Chapter III, the central chapter of the work and clearly the longest, examines the problem from the only perspective through which it might be satisfactorily resolved, that of metaphysical doctrine — not, of course, some more or less 'metaphysical system', the fruit of some philosopher's cogitations and personal opinions, but *the* traditional metaphysics which pertains to the *philosophia perennis* and is a supra-human and infallible doctrine. Also, having in mind readers who might be alarmed by our approach, let it be understood that the metaphysical doctrine of which we speak does not subvert ordinary theology, but strengthens and deepens it. It permits us to attain to the highest meaning of the Marian Mystery, not only with regard to the Black Virgin, but in its fullness, while also offering us the means of defining the symbolism of the black icon, which works at many levels that are only reached within the total substance of this Mystery.

Chapter IV examines an important aspect of the black icon, its connections with alchemy. At the same time it will be possible to establish that the Marian Mystery is included in a prominent way in that much larger whole, the 'Mystery of Salvation', which concerns the whole of human destiny. The final two chapters treat of the spiritual role that Mary plays in this destiny; in Chapter IV we examine a much debated question, whether, within the perspective of 'spiritual alchemy', the Virgin under her black aspect indeed constitutes the 'matter' of the Great Alchemical Work. Finally, in the last chapter, we consider the study of Mary as the prototype of Woman, and her influence as such within that 'spiritual way' that is constituted by the union of man and woman and the Christian conception of marriage. The last pages are admittedly somewhat removed from the question of the black icon, but certainly relate to the Marian Mystery itself, which surpasses this particular point of view. We hope the reader will forgive us and see — or so we hope — the capital importance of this question for the destiny of man, a question we too often neglect to consider from this our chosen point of view.

1

The Black Icon

BLACK VIRGINS are by no means an isolated phenomenon in the history of religious imagery, divine beings with a black face or body being found in many traditions. For example, in ancient Greece we find numerous instances of feminine divinities venerated at certain places or under certain circumstances under this form: for example the black (*melaina*) Demeter of Phigalia, near Bassae in Arcadia, the black Aphrodite honored by the Corinthians, Arcadians and Thespians of Boeotia, and, above all, the Artemis of Ephesus, of whom we shall have many occasions to speak. In Egypt there was a black Isis, mentioned in hieroglyphic texts under the name of 'the black lady', while in India we have the Great Goddess Kali, whose very name means 'the Black'; finally, in the Celtic world there was Dana, Anna or Annis, the 'Black Annis' of Leicestershire folklore. It will have been noted that it is predominantly feminine entities that are portrayed in this way, though black gods do occur: for instance Krishna and Shiva in India, and Osiris in Egypt, who is sometimes called the 'Great Black' (*kem our*), very probably in connection with the sacred bull to which he was sometimes assimilated. We should take care to note, however, that it is only in certain circumstances or under certain relationships that divine beings are shown as, or called, black; more usually they are white. This is an interesting observation, and should be borne in mind, for it is exactly what occurs with representations of the Virgin Mary, and leads us at the outset to think that, even if she is sometimes portrayed as white and sometimes as black, this is probably to emphasize certain of her aspects or attributes.

Having said this, and before addressing the question which is the very purpose of this work, we should first recall, if only briefly, what a Black Virgin is archeologically speaking,; then, how these effigies are distributed geographically, and, perhaps more importantly, topologically; and finally, what their origin is.

So, to begin with, do Black Virgins exist?

What an absurd question, it will be thought, at the start of a book specifically dealing with this type of representation. However, it is not we who put the question, but a well-known specialist in the romanesque art of the Auvergne, Canon Craplet. In *Auvergne romane*, which forms part of the celebrated 'Zodiaques' collection published in 1972, the fiery ecclesiastic had no hesitation in answering that there were never any Black Virgins, only romanesque statues 'in majesty' that were subsequently painted black. It is true he bases his claim on undeniable facts, such as the existence of the Virgin of Orcival, which for a long time was considered to be black until a modern restoration revealed her original light color; and there are some other similar cases. Despite this, Canon Craplet's view is nothing but a whim. It is absolutely certain that authentic Black Virgins do exist, which were black from the start, as is also proved in their case by the archeological study of material and coloration.

Besides, it should be clearly stated that if white statues were blackened, this was apparently to imitate those that were black from the start. We should add, it is very often the case that, when a black statue has disappeared and unduly replaced with a white one, the force of the oral tradition of the faithful has caused them to have this new one blackened, or blacken it themselves.

This in itself is very important, even as important as the existence of authentic black statues, for ours is not the point of view of the archeologist or art historian, whose primary aim is to determine the precise historical quality of the pieces studied; our aim is the study of the sacred, and what counts in this instance is the permanence of the type of the Black Virgin in the Christian West, up to the present, and the very strong attachment of so many of the faithful to this representation of the Virgin Mary. In this perspective, the existence of numerous blackened statues only reinforces the significance of the phenomenon and constitutes a further invitation to investigate it.

Historically speaking, the true Black Virgin goes back to the Middle Ages (eleventh to the thirteenth century). It is a statue of modest proportions; 30cm wide and from 70 to 80 cm high, generally of wood, and often covered with a layer of lime to which the artist applied the colors: black for the face and hands and blue, green, red and gold for the garments.

The most perfect and beautiful type is that of the 'Virgin in Majesty', which is, moreover, identical in composition to the white version. The Virgin is seated on a throne with the Child Jesus on her knees, and both are facing forward: this is the Mother presenting her Son. Traditionally it is considered to represent the Gospel scene of Mary presenting the Child Jesus to the adoring Magi and, through a trans-historical extension, the entire universe. The Child, which has the head of an adult and a priestly mien, is the eternal Logos, hand raised in blessing. The Mother is stiff and stern, with a strange gaze; she does not look at us; it is as though her gaze is lost; it passes through the invisible, or, rather, it is the gaze of the invisible passing through us without seeing us.

This representation, in evidence since the Catacombs, spread widely in the West after being fixed in the East in accordance with the canons established in 431 by the Council of Ephesus, at which Mary was proclaimed Theotokos, or 'Mother of God'.

This type, in size, material, and mien, is very similar in style to the *xoanon*, the cult statue of the Ancient Greeks, an example of which, unfortunately, we no longer possess. However, we can get a very good idea of it from a statue of the Osiris cult, a magnificent Egyptian 'xoanon', a unique piece preserved in the Louvre; it, too, surprises the visitor with its strange gaze. To use different language, we might say that here we are confronted with an *icon*. In his book *La verite des icones*, published in 1984, L. Bouyer quite correctly applied this word to romanesque statuary, to which it applies as much as to the Byzantine pictures for which it is usually reserved. The concept of the *icon* is that of a *sacred* image, dependent on *sacred art*, which is quite different from simply *religious* art. Sacred art essentially aims at, and succeeds in, rendering sensible the invisible behind, and in, visible forms; it is that art which, through the utilization of means placed at the disposal of the artist, makes majesty and transcendence present to us. When the work is successful, the heavenly figure represented so overwhelms us that it completely disrupts our habitual psychic state and, properly speaking, fascinates us, releasing in us that very particular feeling of reverential awe and supernatural joy known to the Greeks as *thambos*. All 'Virgins in Majesty' have this effect upon the beholder; but, with the black 'Majesties', the fascination is twice as powerful. Concerning this we are reminded of a rather significant occurrence. Some years ago, when I went to Mende to photograph the Black Virgin in the chapel of the White Penitents, it happened that I had to ask for the key at the Tourist Office, where I was told I could not go to the chapel unaccompanied. I was dealing with a friendly young girl who seemed somewhat hesitant about accompanying me; when asked the reason for this, I was surprised to hear her say that the Virgin there frightened her. She nevertheless went with me, but on entering, I had an inkling of how that young girl felt, for the 'Black Majesty' enthroned above the altar was particularly impressive, and I must add that without a doubt, the gaze of the statue exercised greater fascination on me than any other I have seen.

Given the high quality of the black images 'In Majesty', should this be considered the only type to qualify as an authentic Black Virgin? Huynen holds this view, and for this reason as well as others, disqualifies most of the two hundred Black Virgins of France, leaving only forty authentic ones. We cannot agree with him, especially because a good many of his dozen other criteria are debatable. We prefer to accept, with Madame Cassagnes-Brouquet, that from the start there were very likely many types of the black statue, given, we repeat, that the imagery of the Virgin was established from as early as the first centuries, and that, alongside the 'In Majesty', we encounter the *Eleousa*, the 'Virgin of Tenderness', where the mother has her head inclined towards the child, a type that derives from the ancient *courotrophos*, or 'nourishing mother'. If statues of Mary conforming to this conception had not existed, it is difficult to understand how Celtic and Isiac statues, which we shall discuss shortly, could be taken for images of Mary.

Anyone interested in Black Virgins is immediately struck by how relatively restricted and very localized is the area where they are found. They are largely confined to Western Europe and particularly France, which possesses at least four-fifths of the known images. Their number decreases as we move toward Eastern Europe, where only a few are found.

Outside of France, Black Virgins are to be found in Germany (Cologne, Altoeting, Maria Zell), the Benelux region and Holland (Dinand, Louvain, and Hal), Croatia (Maria Bistrica), Spain (Avila, Caceres, Guadelupe, Madrid, Monserrat, Saragossa, Salamanca, and Compostella), Hungary (Szekes, Fejirvar, and Gior), Italy (Foggia, Loretto, Oropa), Portugal (Lisbon, Porto), Rumania (Bucharest), Switzerland (Einsiedeln), and Czechoslovakia (Prague). To which we can appropriately add eastern black icons found in Russia (Our Lady of Kazan), Poland (Our Lady of Czestochowa) and Greece (two miraculous Athonite icons: the Virgin Koukouzelissa, of the Great Lavra, and the Virgin Portaitissa, of the monastery of Iveron). Obviously we have only cited the principal examples.

Even in France, where the greatest number and the most famous Black Virgins are to be found, their distribution is clearly defined; they are mostly found in the area south of a line going more or less from Pau to the Ardennes (see Plate I). There are far fewer to the north, even though two famous sites, Chartres and Mont-Saint-Michel, are located there. In the south are two very rich regions: Languedoc (Roussillon and Bouches-du-Rhone) and the Center.

Saillens' research has also shown that apparently Black Virgins are invariably found along the great pilgrimage routes and routes previously followed by the Greek merchants, such as the 'Tin Route', and finally at important Gallic cult sites.

We can also speak of a 'natural setting', where one is most likely to come across the Black Virgin. It is typically elevated (sometimes no more than a simple mound), with a grotto and a spring or well. We should add: harbors.

These sites often strike the least predisposed visitor with their special character, a character which is hard to define, but provokes a sense of some particularly strong 'presence'. These are sacred sites. In fact, places are not defined solely by their materiality—by 'extension', as Descartes and his rationalist successors would have it—but more by their particular 'quality', which is dependent upon factors other than matter, for matter is penetrated by a certain irradiation of the Spirit; and there are privileged places where, as Barres put it, the 'Spirit blows' more strongly than elsewhere. Certain places even have a harmonic relationship with a great archetype, which they manifest by clothing it in a bodily form, which can even be a person.

Such a place is Chartres, where the Black Virgin still sits in majesty in the splendid crypt not far from the original well. Such is Mont-Saint-Michel, that 'acropolis of mists, mystical fortress, reef crowned with prayer, erect in the solitude of sand and sky' (Thierry Maulnier). The paltry Madonna of blackened plaster that the monks of Pontigny placed in the Abbey in the nineteenth century was intended to recall the very old Black Virgin, Our Lady of Mont Tombe, which disappeared in 1790, but was originally placed in the lower crypt or 'Underground Chapel' where, in the eighth century, St Aubert excavated his oratory to St Michael.

Such also is the astonishing site of Le Puy, where volcanic phenomena raised up needles pointing to the sky as if to prepare in advance for the basilicas of the Black Virgin and St Michael. Le Puy is one of the four great assembly points for pilgrims to Compostella.

Such is Rocamadour, formerly called *Vallis Tenebrosa* on account of the deep fault that opens in the calcareous table-land. To the cliff that rises precipitously to nearly 200m above the chasm cling, in descending order, the stronghold, the churches, the chapels and the small town.

'Among the privileged sites of the Western World,' writes Henri Montaigu,

> Rocamadour, that fantastic citadel, a veritable 'Mont-Saint-Michel on land', remains one of the most remarkable testimonies to mediaeval grandeur, to its capacity to translate the sacred deposit into tangible works. . . . Rocamadour . . . set off the main thoroughfares and away from the principal towns, in the middle of a wilderness and on the near vertical flank of a rock, remains one of the strangest manifestations of the mysterious genius of Christianity.

There, in a hollow in the bare rock of the small chapel, one of the most extraordinary Black Virgins still reigns.

Such, finally, is the less spectacular, but very moving Abbey of St Victor at Marseilles, the domain of Our Lady of Confession, the

'Bueno Mero negro', with her crypt in what used to be the small grotto where the first Christians assembled. It was there, near the grotto, that Cassian, in about 415, established the first monastery in the West, dedicating it to Mary and St Victor. The miraculous well in the upper church formerly opened into the crypt, as at Chartres.

These are the most important seats of the cult of the Black Virgin, which in the Middle Ages drew the most pilgrims. In conclusion, let us add, given the importance of the city, the Black Virgin of Paris, 'Our Lady of Good Deliverance', which was formerly in the Church of Saint-Étienne des Grès until the latter was demolished to make way for the rue Soufflot. The modern, but very black image is currently at the Convent of St Thomas de Villeneuve at Neuilly-sur-Seine (see Plate XX). There is also another black statue, at the Convent of Picpus, 'Our Lady of Peace', a reproduction of the 'Virgin of Joys' destroyed in 1793. Finally, let us recall that in 1888 C. Flammarion saw a Black Virgin in the foundations of the Observatory, placed there in 1671 with an inscription designating it as 'Our Lady Under-the-Earth', which would certainly appear to make it a replica of the one at Chartres. All this proves there was a significant cult of the Black Virgin at the capital, which is corroborated by the presence of the Black Virgin at nearby Longpont. The old statue found at the abbey in 1031 has been destroyed, but today there are two others, one of which, from the seventeenth century, is black. This area was probably more or less dependent on Chartres, which is not far off.

The origin of the Black Virgins has been pondered for ages.

In the past it was often said these statues were brought from the East by returning Crusaders. Why? Quite simply because it was thought that all orientals had very dark skin, and that it was thus that they represented persons in their portraits. Obviously this explanation has no foundation at all, and besides, we have nothing, or very little, to warrant this version of the eastern origins of our black statues. No doubt in the East the Crusaders did find statuettes of Isis carrying the child Horus, which could very easily have been confused with one of the Virgin with Child. Let it be clearly understood, however, that in the majority of these cases, neither Isis nor Horus would have been black. Black Isis statues did exist, and we shall need to speak of them, but they were somewhat rare, and if a couple had turned up, this would hardly have constituted a point of departure for the proliferation of Black Virgins that occurred during the Middle Ages. In any case, we have no documentation on the subject. Local tradition, which certainly has its importance, is only affirmative for Mende, Liesse, Ribeauville, and Le Puy. The last mentioned is the clearest instance: when the revolutionaries burnt the former black statue of Our Lady of Le Puy, an Isiac stone placed in the little relic compartment in its back was found in the ashes, which is certainly rather troubling.

But the most important element concerning the origin of Black Virgins is the collection of legends explaining it in terms of a miraculous 'discovery'. Nine times out of ten these statues were found, thanks to a supernatural sign, underground, in a tree, flowering bush, spring, lake, well, or a foundation. And eight times out of ten it was an ox that made the discovery, as happened at Err, in Roussillon, where the effigy was found in a tree trunk thanks to the peculiar bellowing of a bull. Sometimes the 'sign' is more spectacular: at Mauriac, for instance, the statue was found by one of Clovis's grand-daughters. Attracted by a light shining in a clearing, she discovered it on a marble table lit by a candle and guarded by a lioness and her cubs! Here we are clearly within the realm of the supernatural. Sometimes, though, the discovery is quite simple: at Clermont-Ferrand, according to local tradition, the statue was found in the sixth century in the sacred well of the church by the bishop St Avit.

These etiological legends are very important and we shall soon see how to interpret them. For the moment, what should be deduced from them is that the miraculous discovery they report is additional proof of the importance attached to these representations of the Virgin.

Another fact deserving attention is that the vast majority of them appeared during a clearly defined and relatively limited period, the eleventh and twelfth centuries, and this immediately prompts us to ask why they were largely 'found' at precisely that point in time.

But before answering this question, we should first remember that the Marian cult began very early, in the first centuries of our era, in fact, as is proved by the paintings in the catacombs already mentioned. Its prodigious development, however, came after the

Councils of Ephesus (431) and Chalcedon (451), when Mary was solemnly proclaimed Theotokos, 'Mother of God' and all-powerful in her intercession, respectively.

From then on the figure of Mary assumed vast proportions, and this, it should not be forgotten, in a world that was still largely attached to the ideas and forms of the old religion, or rather, old religions, which were still widely practised in Europe, despite the official victory of Christianity. Time-honored ways of thinking and feeling do not change over night. Now, at the time, the most popular beliefs and cults were those addressed to the various forms of the divinity known as 'The Great Mother' or 'The Mother of the gods'. Moreover, the conception of religion in those days differed profoundly from its conception in the modern world, where it constitutes a separate, almost sealed-off domain alongside ordinary life and its problems, and without much to do with them. This was certainly not the case then: in the different polytheisms we encounter what could be called a 'globalizing conception' of human life, according to which religious faith and rites conditioned every domain and activity of life, including the very important and far-reaching ones of material life, especially the exercise of agriculture, which in those days was the principal activity. With different nuances, the same was true for Christianity, and this lasted for the whole of the Middle Ages. To return, then, to the pre-Christian cult of the 'Great Mother' and her various hypostases, we need to remember that their attributes concerned not only the life of the spirit, but, beyond it, the different areas of material existence. Given these conditions, it can be readily understood that among the pre-Christians at the beginning of our era, the equation *Mother of God = Mother of the gods* would quite naturally present itself to, and impose itself upon, their understanding, with the Virgin Mary thus taking on the attributes of the latter. It is probable that for a certain period, before she supplanted the old divinities, she was venerated *alongside* them. This is proved by the situation in India where, even today, the Virgin is venerated by numerous Hindus alongside, and in the same way as, their own Great Goddess Mother, without supplanting her. As for Christians, given the religious mentality mentioned above, they accustomed themselves to admitting that the

Mother of God is, in certain respects and *mutatis mutandis*, able to occupy the place and fill the role of the *Mother of the gods*.

A deciding factor in this evolution was the astonishing resemblance between the representation of the Virgin Mary, which we spoke of earlier, and the various hypostases of the Great Mother. In particular, there was a host of small domestic statues intended for family worship, of the type called 'Virgin with Child', whether referring to Greco-Roman or Celtic divinities. Now, according to the great archeologist Fr. Delattre in his book *Le culte de la Sainte Vierge en Afrique*, it was very difficult to differentiate between a statuette of Isis with the child Horus and one of the Virgin. In his opinion, the only way of doing so was by examining the objects accompanying it, including offerings, to see if they were characteristically Christian. These remarks apply with equal force to the representations of both Greco-Roman and indigenous Celtic divinities, all of them hypostases of the Great Mother. All these divine figures are chthonic, that is to say, connected with the earth, for, by virtue of their femininity, they are the source of both human fecundity and the fecundity of the soil.

Because their worship spread here and there throughout western Europe and Gaul, the Greco-Roman divinities of most interest to us are Demeter (Ceres), Cybele, Isis and Artemis (the Diana of the Romans).

Ceres-Demeter especially presided over crops, and was symbolized by the verdant earth of spring and summer. The principal festival of her cult was the *Cerealia*, which took place from April 12 to 19. She was also celebrated on February 2, the occasion of the sowing of the seed; the ceremony unfolded under torchlight and its substitution by the Feast of Candlemas, by order of Pope Gelasius in 472, is a quite striking example of continuity in the succession of cults. In other respects the personality of Ceres far surpassed the role of a crop divinity, for at that time she was assimilated to the *Magna Mater*, as were all the others still to be mentioned. In this capacity her cult included 'mysteries', exclusive to women, moreover, celebrated in August at the season of the harvest. We can be almost certain it is not by accident that the Virgin is also celebrated during this month, on the 15th, to be precise. Within the same order of ideas, let us remember that the Church of Our Lady of the *Fields* in Paris stands on the foundations of an ancient temple of Ceres. This is not an isolated case; archeology can provide us with many other examples.

Cybele, the Phrygian 'Mother of the gods', whose image was originally a black stone fallen from heaven onto which a face was sculpted, a stone venerated at Pessinonte and transferred to Rome in 205 BC., also presided at famous 'mysteries' comprising a sort of baptism, a sacred meal at which bread and wine were consumed, and a mystical marriage, all of which were deemed to ensure immortality. Cybele was greatly honoured at Ephesus. In the sixth century BC, the Phoenicians took her from there to Marseilles whence her cult spread into southeast and eastern Gaul. Saillens has counted 47 towns where Mary succeeded Cybele: the cult was well established at Lyon, Vichy, and Arles, which possessed a statue of the Black Virgin (now lost); Cybele had a temple there; at Pennes, in Les Bouches-du-Rhone, as late as 1610, a bas-relief of the goddess could be seen on the outside wall of the church; at Limoux, the people call the Black Virgin an 'old sybil' (the mistake is transparent); not far off, at Alet, the church has capitals from the temple of Cybele, who presided at the thermal baths; at Notre-Dame in Paris we find the goddess at the feet of Christ in the central portal; at Monserrat, the Virgin, like Cybele, has a crenelated crown and the Child Jesus holds a pine cone from the tree sacred to the goddess. In conclusion, let us remember that the chief feast of Cybele was held on March 25, the date on which the Annunciation of the Virgin Mary is now celebrated.

But the Phoenicians not only brought Cybele to Marseilles; above all, they introduced Artemis (Diana to the Romans), the Artemis of Ephesus, a black goddess who had her own 'mysteries' celebrated on the heights of the Solmissos.

The ancient statue, or xoanon, at Ephesus was made of ebony, so Pliny the Elder informs us. According to Pausanias, the one at the temple of Laconia was also black, being of the same wood, while that of the temple of Phocis was of black marble. The effigy brought to Marseilles was a faithful replica of the xoanon of Ephesus. During this period, the end of Antiquity and the first centuries of our era, there were two types of Artemis effigies: the famous bobbin-statue

with black head and hands and gilded bobbin body, and the very
widespread courotrophos, or 'Virgin with Child' (see Plate III).

These effigies can definitely be regarded as forerunners of our
Black Virgins. Ch. Picard, the great specialist on the statue from
Ephesus, has noted both in his *Origines du polythéisme hellénique*
and in *Éphèse et Claros*, all the signs that militate in favor of this
opinion, which was already held by Hogarth in his study on *The
Archaic Artemisia*, and apparently as early as 1834 by R. Rochette, who
wrote in his *Discours sur les types imitatifs , , , de l'art chretien*: 'Our
Black Virgins resemble trait for trait the Ephesian Diana according to
material, style, and even the circumstances of their discovery.' The
final words obviously allude to the tradition concerning the original
effigy, which preceded the xoanon. It, too, was a black stone,
probably a meteorite, found in a marsh by the Amazons who raised a
small sanctuary to it. In traditional societies, meteorites were always
considered sacred because fallen from heaven, and, as such, apt to be
bearers of blessings or even, as in this case, inhabited by a divine
being, or at least by its *mana*. In this latter role the aerolith acts as a
betyl, which is a deformation of the Hebrew *Beth-El*, meaning 'house
of God', as stated in the biblical account of Jacob's dream. The favors
of betyls occasionally continue in the Christian world: in the church
of Hagetmau (Landes) are two columns reputed to procure milk for
nursing mothers, and at Agde, in the church of the Genouillade,
stands a feminine betyl of Greco-Roman origin that has a knee-like
imprint and is called 'Knee of the Virgin'. But what is of particular
interest is that the legend of the discovery of the black stone at
Ephesus by the Amazons belongs, as will have been noticed, to that
sort of etiological account which, by alleging the miraculous
discovery of sacred statues, aims to establish their supernatural
character as supports of spiritual influences. This is exactly how the
legends of discovery of our Black Virgins should be understood.

Installed at Marseilles, the black statue of Ephesus became the
tutelary goddess of the city. Would the effigy have been found at the
site occupied by the Abbey of St Victor where today the Black Virgin, Our Lady of Confession, reigns? In all probability, for it is there,
near the little grotto which had become the crypt of the church, that
Cassian established his monastery in 415, dedicating it to Mary and

equipping it with the original statuette, destroyed by the Arabs, which must have succeeded the Ephesus statue.

From 300 BC onwards, and ever-increasingly during the first centuries of our era, the cult of Isis spread throughout the western and eastern worlds, enjoying extraordinary success. The Egyptian goddess had by then, like Cybele and Artemis, become an hypostasis of the *Magna Mater*. Furthermore it is certain that, from the Pharonic era on, Isis was held, at least in certain circumstances and under certain conditions, to be a *black* goddess. A text from the Middle Kingdom (third millenium BC) cited by F. Dumas in his book on the mummies of the Egyptian temples (*Les mammisis des temples egyptiens*), states word for word that Isis was born in the form of a 'black and red woman (*set kemet desheret*), full of life and gentle in love.' Let us recall that when she appeared to Lucius in Apuleus' novel *The Metamorphoses* or *Golden Ass*, she wore a black mantle over a predominantly red tunic; it is thus all the more noteworthy that in the icon of Cambrai, which is counted among the Black Virgins, Mary is dressed in exactly the same way, in a black mantle over a red tunic. In the Greco-Roman epoch, the attribution of the color black to Isis is confirmed by a passage in the XIIth treatise of the Hermetic Writings entitled *The Core Cosmou*, in which Isis herself tells us that

> her grandfather Kamephis ... honored her with 'perfect blackness' ... when he transmitted 'the secret doctrine' to her;

and also in the magic papyri (section VII of the collection of the *Papyri graecae magicae*, 492–503), where we read, for example, this magician's invocation:

> I invoke you, Lady Isis, whom the Agathodaimon has appointed to rule over perfect blackness.

As regards representations, it should not be thought that Isis was always portrayed with a black visage, for this is far from being so, but such representations did exist in Antiquity, as, for example, an Egyptian Isis of the Greco-Roman period modeled in black earth, described by P. Perdrizet in his *Terres cuites grecques d'Égypte de la Collection Fouquet* (see Plate II). At the Paris church of Saint-Germain-des-Prés, which was built on a former Isiac site, a stone statuette of a black Isis was fixed into an inside wall and venerated—therefore considered to be an image of Mary—up until 1514, when it was destroyed by order of Cardinal Briçonnet. According to Witkowski in his *L'Art profane à l'église*, similar statuettes, not always black, it is true, were to be found in the Cathedral of Metz and the church of Saint-Etienne of Lyon; one could also be seen in the church of Ranville (Orne), not far from the Delivrande which at one time possessed a Black Virgin (today white). According to local tradition, this statuette of Isis had been there since time immemorial and would doubtless be there still, if, as at Paris, the local curé had not effected its disappearance in 1757. In 1862 Charles Bigarne, in his *Considérations sur le culte d'Isis chez les Éduens*, mentioned several statues of Isis under the celebrated title of *Virgo paritura*, 'The Virgin about to give birth', which we shall meet again later, and referred to a Latin inscription worded as follows: *Isidi seu Virgini ex qua filius proditurus est*, 'To Isis the Virgin from whom a son shall be born.' There must be many others, as at Longpont for example, in Ile-de-France, where, according to local tradition, the old Black Virgin perpetuated the memory of an Isis. The tradition has it that St Denis, arriving from Rome, explained that Isis was a prefiguration of Mary. Those wishing to pursue this matter further can consult the four volume reference work of Leclant and Clerc, *Inventaire Bibliographique des Isiaca*, published at Leyden, 1972-1990.

Among the traces of the Isis cult in Gaul, we should not forget the place-names that perpetuate the presence of a sanctuary or group of faithful, as, for example, Isse (Loire-Atlantique) and Issy-les-Moulineaux. The form Issy derives from *Isiacum*, which, quite simply, denotes a person who is a mystic of Isis, an 'Isiac'. If we are to believe Fr de Montfaucon, of the Congregation of St Maur, writing in *Les Antiquites nationales*, it would seem the church of St Geneviève at Issy-les-Moulineaux was built on a site formerly belonging to a confraternity of Isis.

In light of the above, we can gauge the enormous impact the Greco-Egyptian cult had on Gaul, as on the whole of western Europe, particularly through its 'mysteries', which were certainly the most noble of those mentioned in this study, and for that reason especially practised by the elite, although not only by them, for we have documentary evidence from a cemetery for legionaries at Trevoux (Ain) showing that a number of these soldiers were initiates of Isis. The same applies to a 'veteran's' residence at Lyon.

Whatever influence these Greco-Roman divinities had upon the cult of the Virgin in general, and the Black Virgin in particular, we should not forget another, no doubt even more important, that of the Celtic divinities, whose cult flourished particularly in the Gallic region, a cult with distant origins going back to the neolithic age (starting from 9000 BC) and even beyond, to the paleolithic. The steatopygous statues of the latter age bear witness to a cult of the *Magna Mater* presiding over maternity and fertility in general. Concerning the dawn of history, we have statuettes of grotto-dwelling Gallic Mother-goddesses discovered in France and preserved at the Musee des Èyzies. It is worth noting that the figures of these goddesses have the same attitude as those of our own Virgins, for example the Gallo-Roman statue discovered at the bottom of a funeral pit near Bernard-en-Vendée (see Plate VII [2]).

The different divine beings encountered in the feminine Pantheon are in reality only different names assumed according to peoples and regions by the *Magna Mater*, who is simultaneously Belisama, Regantona, Brigantia, Bridget and, above all Ana or Dana. Under the name of Belisama she was venerated principally in the Center, the west and the north of the Gaude, as the toponymy here also suggests: Belleme (Orne), Balesmes (Haute-Marne), Blesmes (Aisne), Blismes (Nievre), Beleymas (Dordogne). Particular attention should be given to the shortened form of the name: Belisa, who, through the intermediary Belsa, has given her name to the Beauce, for the Beauce, dear to the poet Peguy, is the country of Chartres, one of the most famous sanctuaries of the Black Virgin, which leads to the conclusion that the *Virgo Paritura* honoured there by the Druids was Belisama, the Great Mother under that name.

We shall dwell a little upon another of these hypostases, that of Anna, whose name also appears in several other forms, such as Ana, Anu, Anis and Dana, which are of little importance to our subject. We shall confine ourselves to Anna, the most interesting in regard to what we are about to examine. Anna is a black divinity, the 'Black

Annis' of Gallic folklore, mentioned at the beginning of the chapter, a black stone effigy of whom is preserved at Montlucon. She is the 'Great Mother of the Bretons' (Goz ar Vretened). Her name has been connected to that of Anna Perenna and Anna Pourna; and with reason: for in Rome, Anna Perenna presided over eating, since the Latin word *anna*, of Indo-European origin, also refers to food. This is also the case in Hinduism, where Anna Pourna signifies 'the goddess overflowing with food.' In both cases, we are in the presence of a power of fecundity in all its forms, without prejudice, moreover, to a role far superior to that of simply providing food— as we shall see.

Anna was venerated throughout Gaul, as the toponymy proves once again: Annegray (Haute-Savoie), Annebecq (Calvados), Anneponte (Charente-Maritime), Annequin (Pas-de-Calais), Anneville (Haute Marne), the fountains of Marianne (Champagne) and Cou-Anne, meaning 'Anna's Hollow', near Châtillon-sur-Seine, and finally Commana (Finistere), which also means 'Anna's Hollow'. In several of these places the Celtic divinity was replaced by St Anne, the most famous instance being the site of Sainte-Anne d'Auray in Brittany, which, long before Nicolazic 'discovered' the statue of the saint there in the seventeenth century, had always been called Ker-Anna, 'the dwelling place of Anna'.

We should also mention that the St Anne of Commana is *black* and, above all, that a black St Anne is to be seen at Chartres, portrayed in a glass window on the north side of the cathedral.

But there is no need to believe that the mother of Mary ousted her daughter in the territories of the Celtic Anna: the Black Virgin reigns in the most important of these, Le Puy, which, during the Gallo-Roman era, was called *Anicium*, that is to say, 'the town of Anis', the other name of Anna, and as late as the tenth century, *Podium Aniciense*, 'Le Puy d'Anicium' or 'Mound of Anicium', whence, through abbreviation, the current name. 'Puy' in this instance denotes the isolated hill, still bearing the name 'Mont d'Anis', to the south of which nestles the town, and from which rises the Corneille rock, bearing a giant statue of the Virgin.

Anicium, like Chartres, was a very important Druidic center, where there remains as evidence a slab of stone called the 'Fever

Stone', thought to have come from a dolmen. Embedded now at the foot of the final flight of steps leading to the entrance of the basilica, it has since time immemorial effected cures. For the rest, archeologists have collected a host of other clues from elsewhere showing that the former mistress of the place was definitely a *black* Anis.

It is remarkable, all the same, that in two of the three most important mediaeval sanctuaries of the Virgin, Chartres and Le Puy, history should lead us back to a black hypostasis of the Celtic Great Mother, and, as we shall soon see, we should no doubt add a third: Rocamadour.

Alongside the *Magna Mater* were certain secondary entities that constituted the so to speak 'small fry' of the great divinity. This state of affairs exists in all polytheisms, where the different attributes of a great divinity are personalized, just as, ultimately, the great divinities themselves are only personifications of the higher attributes of the unique supreme Deity. In the current instance, we find secondary divine entities that are either specifications of the divine attribute of the Great Mother, namely fecundity in its vastest and highest form, or even divine forms better adapted, for some reason or another, to particular regions or places. Thus the whole of Gaul was covered with effigies of those secondary divinities known as the *matres,* the 'mothers', or the *matronae*. C. Jullian, in his *Histoire de la Gaul* mentions the discovery of Gallo-Roman ceramic workshops at Lezoux, near Vichy, and other places, where statuettes and steles of the *matres,* and the Eduen Pistillus in particular, were made, manufacturing them for the whole of Gaul. These *matres* were represented as a triad, one of them, usually the one in the middle, carrying a child, and the other two either a cornucopia or patera. The steles of the Bolands, near Nuits-Saint-George, for example, are like this, as are those of Baux, which are carved on a rock face above a small sanctuary containing an engraved dedication to the 'Three Marys'. In fact, people have not failed to see in the three *matres* a prefiguration of the holy women who, according to tradition, accompanied Lazarus on his journey to Gaul. Obviously, one surmises, a triad of *matres* was venerated at Saintes-Maries-de-la-Mer. It should be clearly understood, though, that the *matres* were not *black*, although at the latter place a black Sarah has been added. This does not prevent their profusely distributed statuary from having influenced the representation of the 'Virgin with Child'.

It is quite possible, as Saillens thinks, that the original feminine deity of Mont-Saint-Michel was Sessia, who gave her name to the now submerged forest of Sessiacum. She was both goddess of sowing and wheat, and a guardian of the dead. This is not at all surprising, for beliefs concerning the dead are everywhere linked to agricultural cults. Moreover, the mountain is called 'Mont-Tombe', which would suggest that it was once the site of a Gallic cemetery, and the Black Virgin, who was called Our Lady of Mont-Tombe, would thus have continued to watch over the dead.

According to local tradition, the personality who reigned over Rocamadour, the third great mediaeval sanctuary, was Soulivia. The name is transparent, being the Latin *Sulevia*, encountered above all in the plural *Suleviae*, denoting Romanized Gallic divinities that, like the *matres*, generally appeared in groups of three, as is borne out by an inscription at Gard, mentioned by Saillens, in which they bear the names *Sulevia*, *Minerva*, and *Iduenna*. Based on this inscription, it would appear that Sulevia, being mentioned first, is the principal entity, which would suggest that at Rocamadour only *her* name lived on in the tradition. At any rate, they were black, chthonic divinities, dwelling in wild places, all of which fits well with Rocamadour, standing as it does above the valley that in the Middle Ages was known as *Vallis tenebrosa* and was reputed to be a terrifying place. The oral tradition of the peasants has it that, long ago, human sacrifices were offered to a 'black mother' called Soulivia, who dwelt in a cavern on the side of the cliff where Zaccheus, alias Amadour, established his oratory and installed the statue of the Virgin Mary. This tradition is especially valuable on more than one count, for it retraces in an exemplary form the sequence of events that must have occurred nearly everywhere where the cult of Mary was substituted for that of a previous mistress. In any event, for the pilgrim of today, eager to go back in time to the origins of our Black Virgins, Rocamadour is without any doubt the most 'telling' sanctuary. There, spanning more than twenty centuries in a moment outside of time, we physically encounter the origin itself, which, so to speak, leaps up before our very eyes. There, towards the back of the cavern of Soulivia, where the bare rock can still be seen—happily it was not covered over with masonry when the oratory was built—we find the current Black Virgin enthroned above the altar, a Christian altar, certainly, but which itself rests upon a Druid altar!

As for the story of human sacrifices offered in honor of Soulivia, it in no way corresponds to reality. A similar story is found in Leicestershire folklore concerning Anna, who was said to be cannibalistic. These 'yarns' do, however, provide the occasion for us to focus on a point of great interest for our subject as a whole. It is long since the history of religions did justice to these highly fanciful accounts, which are baseless as concerns the religious field in question, for the Celts were not practitioners of human sacrifice. As in many traditions other than the Celtic, these accounts are born of an ever-increasingly distorted conception of initiation ceremonies by people who, never having participated in one, remained ignorant of what was involved. Now, as is well known, every initiation arranges its rites according to the schema of 'death and resurrection', rites which aim to make the candidate 'die' to the profane state of fallen man, so that he might live again in a higher one.

Dying to the profane state, the neophyte must return symbolically to the embryonic state before being 'reborn' to the higher, spiritual one. The rites of initiatic death vary, but all aim to effect a *regressus ad uterum,* the regression involved being, of course, not of the physiological but of the cosmological order. In one way or another, the many forms of these rites all use the symbol of the maternal womb, not the womb of the human mother, but of the cosmic Mother, the *Magna Mater*; more often than not this is a submersion in water—a baptism—water being a symbol of the cosmic Womb, or entry into a cave, the cavern-womb of the Earth, of *Terra Mater,* an entry which, like baptism, represents a burial. In other cases, one passes through the belly of a devouring monster—obviously a dummy. In all cases, therefore, what is involved for the candidate is a 'return to the mother', that is to say, to the initiating divinity, who is deemed to kill the individual before causing him to come to life again. As these rites are by definition secret, it is easy to see how gross ideas concerning them could have arisen in the minds of those excluded from them, especially during the intermediate period between the last days of the pre-Christian religions and the definitive establishment of Christianity, when the cults in question were no longer practiced regularly; they would then have easily appeared to be the activities of 'sects', to use a term current today, and the popular imagination, easily fired by things poorly understood, would have concocted all these dark stories in which the chthonic divinities, who, in their caves, were but 'initiatic mothers', became man-eating monsters.

Be that as it may, these accounts have the advantage of proving— not discounting other signs—that the cult of Soulivia at Rocamadour, like that of Anna and, consequently, Belisama, included an initiation or 'mysteries' similar to those of Cybele, Artemis and Isis.

Having set forth the pertinent facts, we shall not hesitate to say that here we are faced with an important aspect of our problem, an aspect to be developed when we address the role of the Virgin in Christian life; but for now, what has just been said regarding the initiatic function of the Greco-Roman and Celtic mothers will enable us to clarify the meaning of a title inscribed above the effigies of certain Black Virgins: *Virgo paritura*, 'the Virgin about to give birth'. The most famous of these inscriptions is that at Chartres, and the current image of Our Lady Under-the-Earth bears, quite legibly, the words *Virgini pariturae* 'to the Virgin about to give birth'. Indeed, the Druidic tradition is well preserved at Chartres, and officially endorsed, since the Cartulary of the Cathedral, *Tractatus de aliquibus nobilitatem et antiquam fundationem Carnutensis ecclesiae tangentibus* says that 100 years before the birth of Christ, the Druids raised a temple to the Virgin who would give birth, and there consecrated a statue of her bearing a child, 'although they were yet to come,' a statue 'that performed many miracles and cures.' The old 1482 missal of Chartres even contains a prayer based on this tradition, thereby integrating it into the religion. But many other Black Virgins have been declared *Virgines pariturae*: Saillens mentions those of Longpont, Auxerre, Châlons-sur-Marne, Nogent-sur-Concy and Moutiers-en-Puisaye. And there are others too: according to the abbot Guibert, the monastery built by him at Nogent-sur-Seine was erected on the site where the Druids sacrificed to *Matri futurae Dei Nascituri*, 'the future Mother of the God to be born.' According to Chasseneux, a similar inscription was to be found in two churches at Bourgogne and in the church at Fontaine-les-Dijon, near the castle where St Bernard was born. Whatever the reality and import of Druid prophetic lore on this subject, a reality and import we in no way doubt, we should mention that the expression *Virgo paritura* has another meaning, linked moreover to the first. It is directly connected with the initiatory role of the *Magna Mater*—always virgin, be it noted, whatever the tradition, even when she has a consort, as is often the case—who most certainly gives birth to a divine child, but who consequently also gives spiritual birth to those admitted to her initiatic cult. This is of utmost importance, for it contains the most plausible and profound explanation for all Marian pilgrimages in general and for the particular popularity once enjoyed, and still enjoyed, by pilgrimages to the sanctuaries of Chartres, Le Puy, Rocamadour and others.

This is because *pilgrimage* is very closely related to initiation; its symbolism, which is that of travelling in general, is always with reference to the archetypal pilgrimage, pilgrimage, that is, to a 'Holy Land', the latter itself being a symbol of the 'Center of the World', the 'place' where one communicates with God On High. In a certain way, according to the case, a land of pilgrimage always incorporates a 'valley of grace' or a 'mountain of salvation', as a copy of the Other World. It is not just any place, but one having been sacralized by a hierophany, where the 'Spirit blows', and where 'heavenly grace', but a grace not unrelated to the 'earth', is manifested and acts with greater power. This is what is sensed more or less consciously by the pilgrims, who go there to be 'recharged', if we may be permitted this expression, with spiritual energy. For the more aware, going to the 'center of the world' is also a means of advancing a little on the 'inner journey' to the 'center of their being', for true pilgrimage is the pilgrimage to the center of being, which is also the 'place of the heart'.

There we have it, a brief outline of the prehistory of our Black Virgins. Given what we have just said about the Gallic divinities, we are compelled to conclude that they are the principal ancestors, which means that the cult of the Black Virgins in western Europe, and especially in Gaul, is *indigenous*. Max Escalon de Fonton strongly defends this thesis in a memorable study in the review *Connaissance des Religions* (vol. IV, 1988) in which he asserts with reason that the Black Virgin was a central symbol of the Celtic priesthood, which was heir to neolithic orthodoxy, and that wherever in Gaul this symbol was alive and *properly understood*, it was Christianized. On the other hand, it is difficult to agree with him when he rejects any connection between the Black Virgins and the Greco-Roman cults of Cybele, Ceres and others, these divinities being, according to him, purely natural, and representing nothing but material and psychic forces that are either natural or human. P. Gordon, who also advocates an indigenous Celtic origin, nevertheless admits that the black effigies coming from the East contributed to the diffusion of the Black Mother image. Who could doubt it? We cannot ignore this influence, which affected more than the plastic representation, as we shall have many occasions to see. Indeed, this is admitted implicitly by M. Escalon de Fonton, at least in the case of Marseilles, which is at the center of his study, when he tells us that there the Greeks preserved the tradition in its totality, and were in contact, at the highest levels of spirituality, with the Celtic and Gallic peoples of the region. It seems to us that the only conclusion to be drawn from this is that if these Greeks, the faithful of Artemis of Ephesus, admitted the doctrine of the Gallic priesthood, it is because they found that it accorded with their own beliefs, which is to say that, for them, Artemis of Ephesus was more than a purely natural divinity. In fact, we do not think the Greco-Roman divinities in question can be thought to express natural forces only, and thus be limited to a purely material domain. In the first place, as we shall see by their very structure, these divinities also had a celestial aspect; secondly, and especially, under the influence of neo-Platonism, Pythagorism, Orphism, and the oriental religions widespread throughout the Roman Empire, the cult had at that time acquired—or recovered—a true spiritual dimension. The most striking case of this is the cult of Isis, but the same is true for many others. J. Carcopino and P. Le Labriolle, for Rome, and Ch. Picard, for Greece, have given many proofs of this 'mystical' renewal of certain cults of the old polytheism. This is why a number of religious elements, such as those we are studying, passed easily into Christianity. With regard to this, it is good to be reminded of what happened in Greece. There the Virgin Mary succeeded without difficulty to the 'Hellenic mothers': she replaced the black Demeter of Phygalia, and Rhea in her temple of Cyzique (Phrygia) in the Peloponnese, and, above all, at Ephesus, became heir to Artemis, a point we shall return to in the next chapter.

This is not the place to pursue this matter further, but the point had to be clarified in order for us to understand and appreciate just how apt are a number of comparisons that in due course shall be made between the Virgin Mary and the Greco-Roman divinities. In any event, it is undeniable that the Mother of God has occasionally seen fit to substitute herself for a previous divinity that could be considered at least as 'naturalistic' as Cybele or Artemis. We have in mind the 1531 apparition in Mexico to the shepherd Juan Diego, at the site consecrated to Tonantzin, the Aztec 'Mother of the gods', who, as Coatlicue, 'She of the Skirt of Serpents', was worshipped as mother of the sun, moon and stars. The Virgin left her image imprinted on the shepherd's cloak of coarse cloth, the same image that has been venerated for nearly 500 years by millions of Mexicans under the name of Our Lady of Guadelupe, the famous Black Virgin of Spain. There is one detail we should not overlook: in this 'achiropite' ('made without hands') image, Mary appears pregnant, which can hardly be called an artistic fantasy!

Having said that, we are in complete agreement with M. Escalon de Fonton when he states that in Gaul the Celtic tradition was certainly foremost and decisive in effecting the transition from the cult of the *Terra Mater* to that of the Mother of Christ, to the extent that, as he further adds, worship among the Gauls was particularly elevated and much closer to the Orthodox Tradition and pure metaphysics than among the Greco-Romans.

This is a good point at which to return to the already mentioned fact that the multiplication of effigies of the Black Virgin extended over a clearly defined period, that of the eleventh and twelfth centuries. This poses a question: if it is true that the black effigies of the Virgin had their origin in the divine statuettes of the first centuries of our era, why did they appear so many centuries later?

For most authors currently occupied with this problem, the determining factors almost certainly derived from ecclesiastical discipline and changes therein. Between the fifth and tenth centuries the Church was involved in eliminating the remnants of the 'pagan' cults and, at the same time, opposed the making of *carved* images, of sculptures, to represent God and the saints. During that period, then, the statuettes of goddess mothers, black or otherwise, that were venerated in secret, were kept hidden, whether they represented the ancient divinities or the Virgin Mary; both instances were surely to be met with. Beginning with the reign of Charlemagne, however, carved images were gradually authorized and the hidden statues reappeared, 'discovered' beneath sites of the ancient cults, in springs, grottoes, sacred trees, etc. where they had been buried or hidden, and were Christianized. Thus it is highly probable that a certain number of black images, having survived the establishment of Christianity, allowed the memory of the chthonic goddesses to be preserved, and constituted the prototypes of the Black Virgins made in the eleventh and twelfth centuries according to the 'majesty' type, canonically fixed at the Council of Ephesus.

These considerations have led certain authors to conclude that the great favor enjoyed by the mediaeval Black Virgins was of popular origin. This is the view of Saillens, for example, and ultimately of S. Cassagnes-Brouquet. The latter would have it as proof that the Black Virgin was the creation of a rural civilization marked by the importance of natural phenomena, such as the earth, grottoes, springs, trees etc. But that is to see only the peripheral aspect of things and to ignore the spiritual dimension of the concept of the Black Virgin; now this is admittedly just the bias of this author, who rejects the mystical interpretations offered him. Besides which, this opinion is untenable; popular creation, in whatever domain it might be, does not exist, above all in the religious domain, where creations are the work of the clergy. This proposition, conceived by the Romantics of the nineteenth century, is baseless. In the question facing us, history or ethnology will be searched in vain for anything to support it, whether it be applied to the pre-Christian origins of the Black Virgins or the development of their cult in the Middle Ages. That the cult was popular, meaning it enjoyed the favor of the people, is certain. But it is no less certain that the people did not invent it, but *received* it.

Another reason occasionally advanced by those who support a popular origin is the fact that the clergy were often opposed to the cult. This is perfectly true, but which clergy is not specified. In this case it is the *secular* clergy, but it is not the same when we turn to the *regular* clergy. Quite the contrary, it is precisely among these latter that the source of the extraordinary development of the cult of the Black Virgin in the eleventh and twelfth centuries should be sought. Most authors today, Escalon, Gordon, Huynen, and Bonvin, agree that it was the work of the great monastic orders, the Benedictines and Cistercians. In this role they are found at Monserrat, Rocamadour, Toulouse and Marseilles, to mention only a few places. The pilgrimage to Rocamadour was created by the Benedictines, as is attested by the *Chronique* of Robert de Thorigny, abbot of Mont-Saint-Michel: the Benedictines were the authors of all the elements present in the legendary and cult of Rocamadour (there is a beautiful book on this subject by Henry Montaigu, *Rocamadour, histoire et geographie sacree du pelerinage*, La Place Royale, 1991). At Toulouse, the cult of the Black Virgin of Daurade appeared with the establishment of the order at the basilica in 1077. Escalon de Fonton, who is perfectly familiar with the problem as it concerns Marseilles, informs us that the abbey of St Victor inherited the ancient tradition from the Celtic priesthood via Cassian, and maintained it, the more so as the abbey was the spiritual authority of the town before becoming a territory of the crown. We hasten to add that this activity connected with the Black Virgins was, of course, part of a much larger undertaking promoting the Marian cult in general, which was to reach its peak with Citeaux and St Bernard, and the dedication of all the great cathedrals to Mary.

It is quite easy to reconstruct the sequence of events: the statues that disappeared, or rather, were hidden, in the fifth century and reappeared in the tenth and eleventh, were the occasion for the monastic orders to introduce both black and white images throughout a vast area of Gaul and Western Europe. The people, who, if not creators, are yet remarkable preservers of antiquities—we have only to think of fairy tales—were the vehicle for the old Celtic and Gallo-

Roman tradition, which at that point reawakened. For their part, the monks were in possession of all the 'knowledge', and 'knowledge' in a traditional society is something quite different from what is understood by the term in the modern world. The knowledge of the monks obviously embraced this latter type of knowledge too, but over and above it they, at least the intellectual elite among them, possessed higher Knowledge of the metaphysical order, and the sacred sciences that flowed from it, such as astrology, alchemy, etc., all of which were also developed in this period under the influence of Spanish sages. It was this intellectual elite that favored the introduction of the cult of the Black Virgin, for they knew very well its lofty spiritual significance stemming from the Celtic tradition. The stereotypical legend of the 'discovery' of the statues indicates an attempt at reactivation; the 'sages' polished up the popular traditions by including them in their high science and prompted the 'discovery' among the people so as to reactivate the cult. In parenthesis, let us specify that we are treating these legends in the way traditional societies would, not as pure fictions, but as accounts transmitting, in a figurative form, realities of an inner order, which, in certain cases, are quite capable of being manifested outwardly in the form of the very images used in the accounts. While not being in a position to pursue this matter further, we are nevertheless keen to make this point. In our opinion, Huynen summed the matter up well in writing (pp 164–165 of his study):

> The Black Virgin is a theological and symbolical construct that was simultaneously introduced everywhere, because it conveyed a philosophical [we would prefer to say: metaphysical] thinking and conception of Mary common to all the contemporary monasteries. . . . Everywhere artists executed a message in wood commissioned by the monastic orders. . . .'

In other respects, this message, in order to be properly understood, needs to be placed within the total contemporary intellectual and social context. During the eleventh and twelfth centuries, we witness a prodigious attempt at general restoration of the Celtic Tradition, grafted onto Christianity, in the social, political, intellectual, and religious domain. What was effected then was nothing less than the definitive constitution of a true Christian society in a spirit perfectly in harmony with the Universal Sacred Tradition, after the fits and starts of the first millenium, thanks to a revival of the richest Celtic elements relating to the primordial tradition as they appeared in the institution of chivalry and the Order of the Temple, and the epic of the Breton Romances with the Quest of the Holy Grail. All this was clearly perceived by the late Fr Louis Lallement in his truly beautiful book *La vocation de l'occident*, republished a few years ago, we are pleased to say. Within this institutional context of fully religious inspiration, the cult of the Black Virgin must have been of particular importance for the great monastic orders to have spread it in the way we have described.

Thus is posed the question of the meaning and role of the Black Virgin and, after the historical summary just given, it is now time to address the heart of our subject. But, as already mentioned, nothing can be said about the Black Virgin without first considering the Marian Mystery as a whole, the former being only one aspect. We already have proof of this in the fact that many of the external traits or details usually presented as characteristic of the Black Virgin belong equally to the Virgin in general, starting with the Marian statue itself, whether 'in majesty' or the 'mother with child'; and the same is also true for the grotto, spring, tree, etc.

Having said this, and just as we are about to begin our study of the Marian mystery, a question arises, suggested by the correspondence of Mary to the divine figures, which, as we have shown, she succeeded. The incontestable fact of this 'succession' nevertheless poses a delicate problem for the Christian who reflects a little thereon. In effect, a choice has to be made between two possibilities. The first is to consider it as having no meaning or, at least, none other than the intention of the Church to replace the old feminine cults she was unable to eliminate completely, and this by substituting another, that of the Virgin, without there being any connection between the two. This is the common view, which a little thought will show to be untenable. The second is to accept that a connection exists, but then the Christian conscience is faced with a problem that is not as easy to resolve as appears at first sight, for it presupposes there to be common elements between the ancient feminine divinities and the Virgin, which, by way of consequence, force us to admit the possibility of a kinship between Christianity, that is to say monotheism, and polytheism. But, the theologian will say, does that not lead us to make of the Virgin a 'goddess'?

This is the problem we shall examine, and in so doing shall discover that, paradoxically, when all is said and done, the difficulty it raises will allow us to further our understanding of the Marian mystery.

2

Regina Mundi

THE POSITION of the Virgin Mary in Christian doctrine and practice is somewhat ambiguous. On the one hand, the Church gives her a lofty rank far above all the saints and has dogmatically declared her 'Mother of God', while on the other, she never ceases to remind us that she considers her to be purely human. What is more, it seems even the title 'Mother of God', which, when one thinks about it, appears exorbitant within a monotheistic context, has yet to receive an entirely satisfactory explanation from speculative theology. It is explained and justified by saying that because Mary is the mother of Christ and Christ is God, she is therefore also the mother of God. But it is rightly felt that this explanation neither gets to the heart of the expression nor exhausts its content. Also, to fully plumb its depths, which are equally those of the Marian Mystery, it would, in our opinion, be more useful to replace provisionally the speculative theological approach with a liturgical one. Liturgical texts, in fact, convey profound intuitions of the faith and open the spirit to regions of knowledge not accessible to theological speculation. We are not thinking only of texts from the Holy Scriptures, chosen by the Church for the various Marian feasts, the value of which is too evident to need insisting upon. We also have in mind creations of a 'literary' order, in the highest sense, such as hymns and prayers etc., composed by highly spiritual persons, which the Church has authenticated by introducing them into the cult, thereby conferring value on them as instruments of knowledge for the faithful; all of which is expressed by the well-known adage *lex orandi lex credendi*, 'the rule of prayer is the rule of faith.'

In order to shed light on the Marian problem as formulated at the end of the last chapter, we shall concentrate upon the various epicleses to the Virgin, that is to say the names under which she is invoked, encountered not only in the biblical texts, hymns, and prayers included in the offices of her feasts, but also, and more especially, in her litanies. These names, of which there are hundreds, reflect the long and unceasing effort of the faithful, supported by the Church, to encompass and express the inexhaustible riches of the personality of Mary. This, in our opinion, is the best way to gain access thereto.

The epicleses we shall be examining belong to the Latin liturgy and the Eastern liturgies of Byzantium and Syria. We encounter them not only in the readings from the Old and New Testaments for the masses and vespers of the Virgin, but also in the anthems, hymns, and motets, such as the *Regina Coeli*, the *Alma Redemptoris mater* and others, and, as already mentioned, in the litanies, those of Loretto for the Latin liturgy, and the Acathist Hymn for the Byzantines. Let us specify, however, that not all the epicleses are of interest to us. A good number, in fact, have only a devotional value—and in saying this we in no way intend to be disdainful, but simply to state that they contribute nothing to the comprehension of the Marian mystery. Those that we shall examine tend rather to have both a poetic and mysterious, even astonishing, air, and it is precisely these that we must examine if our investigation is to make headway.

As has often been said, the incarnation of the Word of God in the virginal womb realized the 'marriage of heaven and earth'; the Christian tradition accordingly has always perceived a close connection between Mary and the earth. In his magnum opus *The Lamb of God*, Fr S. Bulgakov quotes Dostoyevsky's words, making them his own, 'The Virgin Mary is the Mother, the Humid Earth.' In fact woman, mother, and earth are closely related.

The earth is a maternal and nourishing power, the receptacle of diffuse forces, a never-tiring, procreating womb. It summarizes nature, the creative principle of life, in itself, thereby assuming a sacred character, and constituting a hierophany. The sage of Ancient Greece invoked it in the *Core cosmou* as 'Holy Earth, genetrix of all things', and the Sioux wise man, Hehaka Sapa, echoed him in like terms: 'Mother Earth, you are sacred. . . . We have come from you

37

and are part of you.' In fact man feels himself to be a 'son of the earth', like the plants and the trees, having received his substance from her. Does Genesis not explain the creation of Adam in this way? And does the psalmist not sing, 'My substance was not hid from thee when I was made in secret, and curiously wrought in the lowest parts of the earth' (Psalm 139:15)? Whence the personal name 'Demitrius', 'Demitri', which means 'son of Demeter', that is, 'of the Earth'. And if woman feels herself close to the earth, much more so than her companion, it is because she imitates the earth in giving birth and knows how to integrate herself into the larger life of nature; for the earth is not an inert, but a living organism, and has a body composed of soil, stones, mountains and grottoes, the duplicated images of her immense womb. This is why the Virgin Mary is associated with grottoes, and crypts as their substitutes, from the grotto of the Nativity to that of Massabielle. And the earth not only has a body but a soul: the mysterious currents of vital energy running through her. The Earth becomes a person for us, for in man the world and each of its components becomes aware of itself; the earth is also alive, but not conscious; she looks to man to be personalized, and in him she becomes Demeter, the *Terra Mater*.

She becomes eminently so in her who was Woman *par excellence*, the new Eve, and that is why we see her invoked in formulae like the following, taken from the Acathist:

> Rejoice, acquisition of Immortal Fruit!
> Rejoice, laborer that laborest for the Lover of mankind!

This is a tradition that goes back to the first centuries of Christianity, to St Gregory the Thaumaturge, St Ephraim, and others in the East, while in an ancient hymn from the West we likewise find the following two lines in which Mary is completely assimilated to the nourishing Earth:

> Hail, Earth who produces
> The wheat that nourishes.

It is this aspect above all that is particularly developed in the following magnificent texts from oriental liturgies. First we have the anthem which, in the Syro-Maronite liturgy, accompanies the transfer of the Gifts to the altar (it is Christ who speaks): 'I am the Bread of Life descended from heaven to earth that the world might live by me. The Father sent me, Word incorporeal; like a choice grain of wheat in a fertile soil, the womb of Mary received me.' In the Syrian liturgy we find this anthem:

> We glorify Thee, Creator of the world and Ruler of the universe, blessed root that has sprouted and taken its increase from Mary, the thirsting earth, and all creation has been filled with the perfume of its glorious sweetness.

In reading these texts, we cannot help but remember the splendid verses in which Aeschylus, in a fragment from his lost tragedy *The Danaids*, celebrates Mother Earth and her sacred marriage with Heaven:

> Sacred Heaven longs to penetrate the Earth, to delight in this union: like a kiss from the Heavenly Spouse, rain descends upon her, and behold her now who, for mortals, gives birth to the grazing flocks and gifts of Demeter, while the spring flowers bloom under the sparkling dew.

In the passages cited, Mary acquires a cosmic character by virtue of the fact that what is accomplished in her is the marriage of human nature with the divine nature of the Creative Word, and that He whom she brings forth is the Son of Heaven and Earth.

Like the Earth, therefore, Mary is mother, but a *virgin* mother, and when she is likened to the earth it is to a *virgin* Earth: 'Hail, *unplowed* field that produced the divine Ear of Wheat accepted by the whole world' says the Acathist, to which corresponds the hymn of Adam of St *V*ictor:

> *Terra non arabilis* [untilled earth]
> *Quae fructum parturiit.* [which brings forth fruit]

The theme is already found in Tertullian and St Irenaeus who, in his *Adversus haereses*, developed the idea that Mary is the earth of paradise again made virgin so that from it God might form the new Adam.

Thus, in the Acathist and the Syrian hymns, the Virgin has

become Paradise where the Tree of Life is planted: 'Spiritual Paradise having at its center the Tree of Life', and she has even become the Tree itself, 'Tree of tasty fruits that nourishes the faithful,' 'Blessed Tree that has produced the fruit (Christ) giving joy to those who eat of it.' There is no need to be astonished at such a comparison. The tree, which is one of the most universal of sacred symbols, is the image of the inexhaustible spring of cosmic fertility, the image of vegetation, which summarizes everything in itself: cycle of death and resurrection, perpetual regeneration through the vital energy of the earth, it is equally a most fitting symbol of spiritual regeneration, in that, rooted in the earth and with its vertical thrust, it expresses life ascending to heaven. 'The Eden of God is Mary ... from her the Tree of Life issues, enabling exiles to return to Heaven.' Does not Wisdom, who is identified with Mary, say in a passage from the Bible read at certain offices of the Virgin: 'I am the Cedar of Lebanon, the Cypress on Mount Zion, the Palm of Cades and the Plane-tree beside the waters.' The tree was called by its whole nature to be seen as an epiphany of divinity, and more especially of Mother Earth, who therein offers one of her more spectacular productions. Thus it was normal that Mary, too, should also be assimilated to the Tree, and also, naturally, to the Tree of Life; indeed, inasmuch as this latter Tree is in some way an archetype, to all trees.

In the last chapter, we saw that many of the statues were found in a tree or at the foot of one; for example, we have Our Lady of the Three Ears of Wheat near Turkheim, the Virgins of Err and Prats de Mollo in Toussillon, and Our Lady of Tronchaye at Rochefort-en-Terre (Brittany). Fields and forests were home to numerous statues of Our Lady of the Oak. We have already mentioned that the Black Virgin of Longpont (Île-de-France) was originally housed in the hollow of an oak, and the same is true for the statue at Buret (Mayenne), which attracted many pilgrims, the one at Chaville, situated in the forest of Meudon (Île-de-France), and for many others in Picardy, Brittany, and the Bourbonnais. There is also Our Lady of *Roncier* at Josselin (Brittany) and at Lille, Our Lady of Ronzières at Chidrac (Puy-de-Dome), Our Lady of Roumegoux in Albigeois, and Our Lady of Romigier, the Black Virgin of Manosque. These last three names are synonyms of *roncier*, meaning 'bramble bush'.

There is even Our Lady of the Pine, of the Willow, and of the Box-wood. Finally, we should not forget Our Lady of the Pillar at Sara-gossa and Chartres, the second being on that cathedral's left aisle. Both are examples of Our Lady of the Tree, for a pillar, in whatever material, obviously represents the trunk of a tree. We would espe-cially like to draw attention to the Black Virgin of Foggia (see Plate V [2]), in Italy, who is so to speak joined to the tree, which is all the more interesting in that this representation perpetuates the mem-ory of an authentic apparition.

In fact, all vegetable life falls within the domain of Mary: fields, crops, vines, and flowers. This is why the color green has sometimes been assigned to her. The statue of Our Lady of Good Hope at Dijon wears a long green tunic; according to the descriptions of Faujas, the original statue at Le Puy wore a robe the upper part of which was blue-green; at Marseilles, Our Lady of Confession has a black and green dress, and on the Feast of Candlemas, on 2 Febru-ary, the procession is held with green candles; the statue of Our Lady of Murat is dressed in green for the same feast.

The *Song of Songs*, the source of so many of the themes developed in meditations on the Virgin and in the hymns and invocations in her honor, has furnished a particularly celebrated one, that of the 'Walled' or 'Enclosed Garden', evoking those gardens of the East where, secreted behind high walls, exquisite, delightfully scented plants abound. In a sermon that serves as the lesson for the office of 8 December, Paschasius Radbertus, a ninth-century author, says of Mary, 'One sings of her in the *Song of Songs* (4:12): Closed Garden, Sealed Fountain, what issues forth from you is Paradise. Yes, indeed, a garden of delights; every kind of flower and all the perfumes of the virtues are there gathered.' In the Middle Ages, the theme of the Enclosed Garden enjoyed a great vogue in the illustration of 'Books of Hours', which depicted the Virgin in a heavenly orchard. The Byzantine offices of September 7 and 14 acclaim Mary in the follow-ing terms: 'Luminous Garden', 'Living Garden', 'You are the mystical garden that without cultivation has brought forth Christ.'

If Mary is the garden, she is obviously the flower as well, and the following declaration of the young heroine of the *Song of Songs* (2:1) has also been attributed to her: 'I am the flower of the field,

41

and the lily of the valley.' And we see why the month of May has been consecrated to Mary, for it is then that all vegetation bursts forth and gardens are covered with the first flowers. All of this is significant, for the flower is charged with a very rich symbolism, which is similar to that of the tree; like it starting from a seed, it pushes through the earth where it was buried, and raises itself on a vertical stalk to blossom as it gazes at heaven. It was therefore perfectly normal to see therein an image of the Virgin. Thus, she is invoked in the Acathist litany as 'Rose Divine', and in the litanies of the Western Church as 'Mystical Rose', *Rosa mystica*, while the liturgy places Wisdom's words in her mouth: 'I am . . . the Rose of Sharon,' and St Peter Damian calls her the 'Rose of Paradise'. A manuscript from the Bibliotheque Nationale in Paris, the *Rosarius* 12483, deals with the flower mysticism of the Virgin in the Middle Ages. Raymond of Capua recounts that St Agnes of Montepulciano had a joyous vision of the Virgin Rose and we know that at Lourdes, just before the first apparition, Bernadette saw a trembling wild-rose, which remains to this day. It seems floral symbolism attains its highest power with the rose: destined to be the *rosa mystica*, the rose expresses the realization of the possibilities contained in the seed and, thereby, spiritual realization. It is at the same time the symbol of supreme divine knowledge, *mystica*, and of pure love. In Cantos 21 to 23 of the *Divine Comedy* the rose marks the heavenward progress of the elect, and, in Canto 30, Dante perceives the saints and Paradise itself as forming an immense rose.

We saw earlier that the Eastern liturgies compare the Virgin to a field where Christ has germinated like a grain of wheat to feed the world. But Mary gives not only spiritual nourishment, her Son, she also watches over the earthly nourishment of her children. Christian piety has long understood this, entrusting her with the success of the crops, whence 'Our Lady of the Fields', 'Our Lady of the Wheat', 'Our Lady of the Harvest', and 'Our Lady of Bread'. The liturgy itself is not above celebrating her role as protectress of humble works. On 15 May—note the date—the Byzantine liturgical calendar honors 'Our Lady of the Seeds', and the office includes the doxology, 'Oh Christ, Word of the Father, you fell like rain on the field of the Virgin, and, as a perfect grain of wheat, appeared there where no seed had been sown and became food for the world.' We should also mention all the small or para-liturgies of the people, for example, the annual offering of the harvests in Aire-sur-la-Lys to 'Our Lady, Source of Bread' (*Notre-Dame Panetière*), and the offering of the last cut sheaf, practiced in various provinces such as Poitou, Berry, Beauce, and elsewhere. Moreover, we would be wrong to think the Church disdains these popular liturgies; on the contrary, she has always encouraged them, or did so at least until a certain date, as witnessed by this prayer composed in the eleventh century by St Peter Damian:

Oh All-good, All-powerful, with a single word command the hail to neither batter nor ruin us.... Still the storm, restore calm weather, give us warm light, that the clouds might vanish.

The same practices were repeated at the grape harvest, for is not wine, together with bread, the living symbol of the celestial nourishment just mentioned? In Champagne, a statue of 'Our Lady of the Vines' towers above a vine-plant, and many regions have, or used to have, processions bearing a statue of Our Lady decorated with grape clusters. Like wine, the grape vine is the vegetable expression of immortality; in the Near-East it has often been considered a synonym for the Tree of Life. And the liturgical invocations to Mary coincide with those already mentioned, in which the Virgin is likened to a tree: 'Oh Mother of God, you are the true vine bearing the fruit of life,' 'Vine that has offered the cluster of blessings to those that drink of it,' 'Vine that has produced the wine that rejoices souls.'

These invocations, it will be noticed, refer to an essential role of the human mother: that of nourisher, which goes back to that of the Cosmic Mother, Mother Earth. Whence also a title encountered chiefly in Brittany, 'Our Lady of Milk', who gives the precious beverage to nursing women; 'Our Lady of the Marshes' at Fougères, 'Our Lady of the Breast' at Lorienté, 'Our Lady of Treguron' at Gouézec, and others. Another prime attribute of the mother is fecundity, and on this account the Virgin is invoked on behalf of sterile women, or to procure an easy delivery. Thus, at Toulouse, 'fertility belts' are consecrated to the Black Virgin of la Daurade for the successful delivery of those in confinement. Moreover, in the Middle Ages there was no hesitation in representing the Virgin as pregnant or parturient, as at Cucugnan (Eastern Pyrenees), or at Issoire; very few such representations remain today, the most interesting example being that of the Black Virgin of Dijon, 'Our Lady of Good Hope', who is shown with a rounded abdomen and heavy breasts (see Plate XVII).

The fecundity of the Virgin also extends to animals: she protects and ensures the well-being of domestic flocks and herds, whence prayers for, and blessings of, flocks and herds on 15 August in Forez and Aubrac. On the same date, stables are blessed at Elne (Eastern Pyrenees) to prevent contagious diseases. The most spectacular example is that of Our Lady of Vassivière, in Auvergne, whose statue follows the rhythms of the seasonal migration of the herds. In spring, the Black Virgin protectress, together with the herds, ascends from the church of Besse to Vassivière, high up in the mountains, where the Virgin has a chapel in the summer pastures; in September, she re-descends along with the herds. All this is related to the bovine theme, which plays an important role in the Marian cult. As we saw in the previous chapter, the legends of discovery have it that bullocks have led to the discovery of many statues of Mary. Such was the case at Err in Roussillon, at Bollème, at Manosque, at Villedieu, near Saint-Flour, at Lantenay in the Dijonnais, at Bourisp in the Pyrennees, and at other places. At Sarrance in the valley of Aspe (Eastern Pyrenees) it is recounted that, in times past, a bull would swim across the mountain stream each day to go and kneel before 'a stone representing the Virgin', which the people called 'Our Lady of the Stone', and which ensured the fertility of the fields.

This last trait merits attention: it leads us back to fecundity, for the bull is a powerful manifestation of the vital force. It has been noted that the association of the animal with the 'legends' of the Virgin can be justified by the fact that it is also associated with the scene of the Nativity. While this thesis should not be rejected, it seems, rather, that in this instance the animal corresponds to virile power acting upon the 'femininity' of the earth. At this point, a possible transposition can be made to the virginal conception by the celestial power, the latter, in this case, represented by the bull, which is altogether plausible. Be that as it may, the liturgy seems to support this idea, since, in the Acathist litany, Mary is celebrated as the 'Cow that has brought forth the unblemished calf.' Finally, we should note that the constellation of the Bull is the second sign of spring, falling exactly in the period 20 April to 20 May, that is, largely in the month of May which, as we have seen, is related to the Virgin. Moreover, this sign is an earth sign corresponding to telluric fecundity. Later, we shall return to its significance as it bears upon our field of study.

The body of the earth, we have said, is shot through with currents of living energy, but also with other currents of life, currents of water. Spring and fountain, just as the earth itself, are images of the mother, and hence of the Virgin. 'Living and incorruptible source' says the Acathist, 'Inexhaustible source of living water'; 'Oh Mother of God, you are the lively spring gushing forth abundantly.' This is the 'sealed fountain' of the *Song of Songs* recalled above. From the first centuries, as can be confirmed, for example, in the *Arabian Gospel of the Infancy*, Mary has been likened to the *Fons Vitae*, 'Source of Life', the infinite Source, cause and principle of growth, and has inspired the icon of the Virgin *zoodotes peghe*, 'life-giving source', in which she is shown seated with the Child in the basin of a fountain from whence the water falls into a pond around which the blind and lame gather to await healing. This is because water is the original medium of beings, the receptacle of seeds and the matrix of the possibilities of existence; water, together with earth and woman, constitutes the anthropocosmic circuit of fecundity.

The wells consecrated to Mary found in many old churches represent the 'Sealed Fountain', the 'Fountain of Life'. We have already mentioned the well in the crypt at Chartres; at St Victor of Marseilles the well was originally in the crypt, but is now found in the upper church; at Chauriat (Auvergne), the old parish church was built above a crypt with a flowing spring, while the church at Avioth has a miraculous spring under it; at Saint-Germain-des-Prés, in Paris, the well was at the back of the old sanctuary, as it was at the old church of Saint-Marcel; the well still exists at 'Our Lady of the Pine' in the Marne, and, significantly, is called 'Well of the Virgin'; finally, at Our Lady of Limoux, in the Aude, it is in the middle of the choir.

We have already mentioned that several statues of the Virgin were found in wells or springs. At Clermont, the Black Virgin was taken from the miraculous well of 'Our Lady of the Port'; the same occurred at Chappes, Plancoet, and elsewhere. On the subject of miraculous wells, the one at Limoux bears the following inscription: *omnis qui bibit hanc aquam, si fidem addit, salvus erit*, 'whoever drinks this water and has faith, will be healed', for the water in question has curative powers. And does the Virgin not preside over thermal waters, too? We know of 'Our Lady of the Infirm', at Vichy, 'Our Lady of Ax-les-Thermes', 'Our Lady of Bourbonne', 'of Plombières', and many others, for example, at Orcival, Font Romeu, and Liesse, and in large numbers in Brittany: at Folgoet, Baud, Lansoch, Landivy, and elsewhere.

What a contrast with the following epicleses that refer to the symbolism of fire: 'Hail, fiery chariot of the Word', 'Hail, column of fire burning for those in darkness', 'Hail, burning bush, unconsumed.' This last symbol is borrowed from the famous scene in which Yahweh appeared to Moses (Exod. 3:2), which, from very early on in the eastern tradition, became a sign of the virginity of Mary: God hides Himself in the bush of flames that does not burn, but keeps its integrity; in the same way the divine Word was enclosed within the virginal womb while leaving it intact. But Marian piety has especially drawn its poetic images from the stars. This is an occasion to remind ourselves of how sensitive the men of past centuries were to the beauty of the heavens. Greek and Roman poetry is full of elaborations on the theme of the diurnal and nocturnal skies and the stars, a theme further developed during the Middle Ages. These men knew by nature how to lift their heads to the heights as becomes those who, providentially gifted with a vertical posture, are normally led to direct their gaze to the heavenly abode, or at least such was the case prior to the mechanical and materialistic age, which persistently turns our eyes earthwards, no longer letting us read 'the heavenly signs'. For us, the whole poetry of heaven, especially that of the night skies, is encapsulated in the following beautiful line from Euripides' *Electra*:

Oh sable night, nurse of the golden stars!

Thus, a Candlemas hymn of Lauds calls Mary, 'Glorious among the Virgins, sublime among the stars.' Mary had earlier been compared to the moon, with reference to a passage from the *Song of Songs*, which has furnished so many of the texts for the anthems of the offices; all those of the 'Common of the Virgin' are drawn from it. For example, 'Who is this who appears like the dawn, who is beautiful as the moon?' Still more significant is the fact that Mary is represented as standing on the crescent moon, in conformity with the passage from *Revelations* (chap. 12): 'A great sign shall appear in heaven: a woman clothed with the sun, the moon beneath her feet and a crown of twelve stars upon her head.' We shall return to the sun and the stars later; for the moment let us examine the meaning of the moon.

Traditionally the moon symbolizes the rhythms of life; it increases and decreases, disappears and reappears, its life being subject to the universal law of becoming, which includes not only death but also resurrection, the latter being represented precisely by the crescent. The moon controls all the cosmic planes ruled by cyclical becoming; for instance, the waters, vegetation, fertility, the tides, and the fecundity of women, and hence its connection with the already encountered sign of the Bull, which is the second sign of spring and, significantly, the 'the place of exaltation' of the moon.

Christian thought, which is heir to that of antiquity, has long meditated on this theme and applied it to the mystery of Christ and his mother. According to this line of thought, Christ is the sun, but the light of the Christ-Sun only reaches the dark earth through the maternal intervention of Mary (and the Church), for the moon is the symbol of that being who welcomed the light in a motherly way and humbly received it; childbirth and prosperity on earth follow the rhythm of this maternal moon.

Around this theme developed a sort of myth of the 'marriage of the sun and moon'. *Luna*, made pregnant with the light of *Sol*, becomes a mother and engenders all that lives. In silence and obscurity the 'new moon' converses with her fiance; this is the mystical discourse of the Pythagorean 'harmony of the spheres', mentioned by Plutarch in his treatise *On the Face in the Moon*: 'At all times Selene traces circles of love about Helios, and from him, through their union, she receives the power to give birth'. Thus the moon is the intermediary, or mediatrix, between the sun and the earth. Her role is to soften the force of the light by adding to the 'fire' of the sun the 'water' of her being, the 'celestial water of the moon', the 'celestial dew', where the 'warm' and the 'wet' are mixed to engender the creative principle of life on earth.

With this as starting point, Christian thought went on to consider the Christmas sun and the moon: Mary gave birth to the Sun of Justice and became his 'mirror', *Speculum justitiae*, 'Mirror of Justice', as the Litany of Loretto calls her; during the night she leads the choir of the morning sun; she is the Moon with whom the Sun is united in the self-annihilation of his nocturnal incarnation, and thus she is the mother of all that lives.

Also belonging to this theme are the epicleses likening her to the dawn: 'Who is this who appears like the dawn?', 'Dawn of the mysterious day', 'Luminous dawn', as well as the epicleses referring to Mary as the 'Door of the Sun'. In the motet *Ave Regina coelorum*, she is greeted as follows: *salve porta ex qua mundo lux est orta*, 'Hail, door through which light has risen on the world', and in an anthem for the office of 8 September in the Byzantine rite, 'She is the eastern Gate prepared for the entrance of the Great King,' referring to the 'eastern gate' of the Temple at Jerusalem, always closed and reserved for theophanies of Yahweh; but, as we were saying, it also, and in the first place, refers to the 'door of the sun', the point at which the sun rises in the East, and more particularly the 'solstitial door' of Christmas through which the sun, in the depth of the night of winter, enters to resume its ascent. Connected with the same idea are the litanies invoking the Virgin as *Stella Matutina*, 'Morning Star'; appearing at early dawn, this star, which is really the planet Venus, announces the rising of the sun. The Acathist also celebrates Mary, saying, 'Hail, star that leads Christ, the great sun, into the world.'

When the symbol of the 'door' appears in the litanies in the short form *Porta coeli*, *Janua coeli*, it has a different meaning, signifying that Mary is the door of heavenly Paradise, as St Peter Damian declares in this hymn for the Advent season:

The Virgin pregnant with the Word,
Becomes the door of Paradise:
She has brought our God to earth
And opened Heaven's gate to us.

And this takes us back to the theme of the moon and the lunar image of Mary. In order to be understood, the expression *Janua coeli* must once again be viewed in the context of the ancient system of the Cosmos, arranged according to seven ascending planetary spheres. The first of these is the moon, which separates the world below (for this reason called the sublunary world), subject to the cycles of becoming, from the higher spheres, including that of the sun, which share in the permanent and divine life of 'heaven' in the religious sense. In this perspective the moon is called *Janua coeli*, for it is the point of passage from the lower to the divine world. It will no doubt be remembered that in the heavenly ascent of the *Divine Comedy*, Dante correctly placed Purgatory, which, for repentant sinners opens the way to the sun, the Milky Way and the 'Supreme Circle', in the sphere of the moon. Already in Plutarch's treatise, cited above, we find the just sent there to be purified so as to be in a fit state to ascend to the home of the gods. By making Mary the *Janua coeli*, the aim is to emphasize the immense role she plays in the way of salvation, not only because she has given birth to Christ, the author of salvation, but also because she continues to help man in his journey along the path. In the figure of the Woman of the Apocalypse recalled above, the Virgin—for it is she—is stationed above the moon and clothed with the sun; she gives birth to men and enables them to pass from the terrestrial world of mortality to that of eternity. We shall have many occasions to return to this theme.

We have just mentioned the invocation *Stella matutina* found in the litanies. Another, which opens the well-known motet *Ave maris stella*, 'Hail, star of the sea', places Mary at the highest point in the 'field of the stars', for the 'star of the sea' is the pole star, called in Byzantine prayers the 'never-setting star' because it is always stationary, thus determining the *Axis mundi*, the cosmic pole around which the heavens revolve. Because of this, the pole star became a very important symbol in all religious traditions. From the practical point of view it serves to determine the orientation of travellers, especially of those traveling by sea, whence the appellation 'star of the sea', which refers to the role of Mary as patroness and protectress of sailors. Her sanctuaries, particularly those that shelter or once sheltered a Black Virgin, include that at St Victor at Marseilles, where at Candlemas the famous *navettes*, cakes shaped like little ships, are distributed in honor of the 'Good Black Mother', the patroness of mariners; at Boulogne-sur-Mer where, according to the founding legend, the statue arrived in a self-guided boat; at Mont-Saint-Michel, where the Lady Chapel is dedicated to *Stella maris*; and at Rocamadour, where the chronicles refer to numerous miracles involving the shipwrecked.

Mary is to be found in yet another region of the starry heavens, the sixth sign of the Zodiac, called, precisely, 'The Virgin.' This designation, however, does not derive from Mary herself, but from the Virgin Astrea, who belongs to Greco-Roman mythology, and whose legend is related by Hesiod and Aratus. In his *Phenomena*, the latter relates that the Virgin Astrea, incarnation of Justice, lived among men in the Golden Age. In the Age of Silver, however, when humanity began to lose its primordial innocence, she retired into solitude. In the Age of Brass, she left earth, which had become infested with sin, and established herself in Heaven near the constellation of Bootes, where she holds the splendid Ear of Wheat (the Ear, *Spica Virginis*, is the principal star of the sign). The whole of this legend was developed in neo-Pythagorean circles, particularly at the time of Augustus, and especially by P. Nigidius Figulus, the grand-master of the brotherhood during his reign. The renewal inaugurated by Augustus gradually led to the belief that his reign could well usher in something like a new Golden Age, a belief echoed by Virgil in the famous IVth Eclogue of his *Bucolics*, where he celebrates the return of the Virgin Astrea:

> The great cycle of ages begins again:
> The Virgin returns, returns the reign of Saturn.

The whole poem is steeped in the atmosphere of the neo-Pythagorean circles to which Virgil belonged, where the regeneration of humanity was believed to be imminent. To the mystically-minded of Virgil's time, this epoch was truly the end of the 'Great Year', the painful transformations of which would give birth to a new Golden Age, along with the return of Astrea, the Virgin of Justice.

If we dwell at some length on this subject, it is because the Middle Ages always saw a connection between Mary and the 'prophecy' of Virgil on the one hand and the constellation of the Virgin on the other. Abelard, in his *Seventh Epistle*, stated that Virgil, in foretelling the marvelous birth for the consulship of Pollio, had wished to call humanity to rejoice in it as at the announcement of its redemption. In fact, the belief that Virgil foretold the Christian era and that the 'Virgin' of the IVth Eclogue was the mother of Christ, goes back to the first Christian centuries: Phylargyrius, commenting on verse six, writes: 'The Virgin: that is to say Justice or rather, Mary.' Greek Christianity has a tradition handed down by Eusebius, that Constantine had verse six, 'The Virgin will come, leading the king of our desires,' amended with a note stating that the Virgin was Mary. And the Middle Ages as a whole went along with the idea, treating Virgil as an authentic prophet equal to those of the Old Testament; undoubtedly, this was not wrong.

As for the constellation of the Virgin, it plays an important role in the Marian cult, primarily in the calendar of feasts. In March, it appears in the east; during April, May and June it arises in the south; and from July to September it then descends towards the west. In addition, the sun enters the sign of the Virgin on 23 August and remains there until 22 September. We immediately note that the principal Marian feasts occur precisely during these periods: 25 March, the month of May, 15 August, and 8 September. Let us also note the astonishing connection between the sign of the Virgin and the establishment of certain Marian sanctuaries. The great cathedrals, all dedicated to Our Lady, that were built in the twelfth and thirteenth centuries in northern France—in Champagne, Picardie, Ile-de-France, and old Neustria—are situated in such a way as to reproduce almost exactly the constellation of the Virgin on the ground. Thus, the star *Spica* is at Reims, *Gamma* at Chartres, *Delta* at Amiens, and *Epsilon* at Bayeux; the small stars correspond to Evreux, Étampes, Laon and Notre-Dame de l'Épine (a small star near *Spica*). (See Plate VIII)

This should not astonish us, for we know that all traditional peoples often situated their sanctuaries and important towns according to the projection on earth of a particular section of the heavenly map, a projection corresponding, of course, to a precise symbolism, of which the above is an example. The beautiful works of Jean Richer have thrown abundant light on this aspect of sacred geography as it concerns Greece and Rome. This way of doing things stems from the conviction, altogether justified of course, that all parts of the world are in 'sympathy', and that, in outlining their relationships, it is important to be aware of the unity of the cosmos, and, particularly in the case under consideration, to 'capture' the benefic influences descending from heaven to earth.

All these considerations concerning Mary and the stars justify the well-known invocation addressed to her in many motets of the Office: *Regina Coeli*, *Regina Coelorum*, 'Queen of Heaven', 'Queen of the Heavens'. We are reminded yet again of the celestial Woman of the Apocalypse, iconographically depicted by the dark blue mantle covered with stars often worn by the Virgin. And is it not because she is 'Queen of Heaven' that Mary has also been compared to a bird, especially the dove? Once again borrowing their praises from the *Song of Songs* (2:10; 6:8), two anthems of the Magnificat for Vespers of the Feast of the Apparition of Our Lady at Lourdes on 11 February say: 'Come, my hidden dove' and 'This is my dove, my perfect, my immaculate.' This comparison goes back a long way, for we find it in the oldest known prayer to Mary, published by Reizenstein, in which she is proclaimed 'the Dove who has snatched mankind from death.' And from the Acathist we have the following as an explanatory gloss: 'Dove who has given birth to Mercy.'

If now we recapitulate all that has been said concerning the epicleses of the Virgin, we shall notice that these latter refer, in the order we have followed, to the *Four Elements* constituting the visible universe, namely Earth, Water, Air and Fire, so that the figure of Mary that emerges appears to cover the whole visible world, but a world that she dominates, as indicated in these additional invocations: *Regina mundi*, 'Queen of the World', from an anthem for the Feasts of Our Lady of Mount Carmel and the Seven Sorrows of the Blessed Virgin Mary, and 'Empress of the Universe', from the Byzantine liturgy. The whole of Christian consciousness was formerly very much alive to this universal dimension of the Mother of God; a poet like Villon recalls it in his famous ballad, expressed according to the traditional tripartite schema of the structure of the world:

> Lady of Heaven, Regent of the earth,
> Empress of the infernal marshes.

And the great rose of the facade of the Cathedral of Notre-Dame in Paris places the Virgin at its center with the Zodiac on the outer circle, which is a way of proclaiming that Mary is indeed the Empress of the World, for she sits at the Center, the point marked by the *Axis mundi*.

These invocations testify to the efforts made by inspired authors and sages to express symbolically the unfathomable riches of the Virgin. We are aware that modern minds are sometimes scarcely able to grasp the scope of this undertaking, and especially are tempted to dwell on what they consider to be so many incongruities. To take but one example, how do we reconcile the idea of Mary's being the 'earth' and, at the same time, the 'moon' or the 'star of the sea'? We should not, however, attempt to co-ordinate the different symbols in a system that would rationalize them, for that would be to destroy them. In fact, they do not share a *logical coherence,* but an *ontological convergence,* which is far more interesting; for each symbol—and obviously we mean authentic ones, and not allegories—is, over and above its specific determination, an image of the All, a microcosm virtually containing the macrocosm. When, as here, they are presented in a vast array, they do not form a multiplicity that can be added together in a linear sequence, but a multiple unity, like the irradiating lines spreading from a center—the object or being to be qualified—and leading back to it, be it in an asymptotic fashion. The aim of all the cosmic symbols we have surveyed is to help us apprehend something of the Marian mystery. They are the necessary mediators that enable us, by using images from the sensible world, to arrive at the intelligible, other than by abstract concepts that are unable to touch the heart.

As 'Queen of the World', Mary is also *Virgo potens,* 'the powerful Virgin', with a power she uses maternally on behalf of mankind. She

is *Auxilium christianorum*, 'Help of Christians', a help that intervenes in all circumstances, and first of all in a domain where today
we are not accustomed to encounter it, that of *war*. Nevertheless,
the liturgy has not ceased celebrating her as a fearless warrior, 'terrible like an army arrayed for battle' (Anthem for Vespers of 15
August). An anthem for the Feast of Our Lady of the Rosary calls
her 'Virgin of Majesty and Power, Tower of David, whereon hang a
thousand bucklers and all the shields of mighty men', yet another
invocation taken from the *Song of Songs* (4:4). The image of the
'Tower of David' is also found in the Litany of Loretto, while the
Acathist proclaims Mary the 'Fortified Tower', 'Impregnable Ram-
part', 'Strength of Combatants', 'Help of Warriors', 'Thunderous Terror of Enemies', and 'Lightning that strikes down enemies.'

The memory of her interventions lives on, which has led to her
being called 'Our Lady of Victories' in several places, at Thuir, for
example, where at the time of Charlemagne she put the Saracens to
flight. During the course of the Reconquest, Peter II, the king of
Aragon, had the image of the Black Virgin of Rocamadour painted
on his standards, for it was to her that he owed the great victory of
Las Mavas de Tolosa, in 1212. The Black Virgin of Chartres delivered
the city from the besieging Normans; at Dijon the Black Virgin, Our
Lady of Good Hope, protected the inhabitants from a Swiss invasion in 1513; the Black Virgin of Czestochowa forced the Swedes to
lift the siege of the city in 1655, and in 1683 gave Jan Sobieski victory
over the Turks. The most spectacular miracle in this domain is
without doubt the defense of Constantinople, besieged by the Per-
sians in 626. On 7 August the city, defenseless apart from a weak
garrison commanded by the Patriarch Sergius, was attacked while
the emperor was absent from his capital. The Patriarch placed the
soldiers on the ramparts and had them chant the office of the
Acathist—the source of so many of our cited invocations—upon
which the Virgin appeared and, raising her arms, repulsed and
routed the enemy. At daybreak the apparition disappeared and the
enemy was gone. The Patriarch immediately proclaimed the Virgin
'Invincible Strategy' and 'Queen of the Capital', and decided that
in memory of this glorious episode the Acathist be chanted annually on the fifth Saturday of Lent. What is more, the miracle was

repeated several times when the imperial armies displayed banners bearing the image of the Virgin.

The latter is, therefore, quite obviously the protectress of cities, like Marseilles, Lyons and others, and even of roads, whence the representations of castellated Virgins, that is to say wearing a crown composed of elements representing fortified ramparts. There are two reasons for this detail. The first is that the liturgy has likened Mary to a city, more precisely to *the* City, the Holy City; she is called 'City of the universal King', 'City of God', 'City of the Lord, where flow the rivers of blessed Life' (we recognize here the assimilation to Paradise, already mentioned). The second, more fundamental, reason, which explains the first, pertains to the statue itself of the Mother: in traditional thought, the city is likened to the protective maternal womb, hence the fact that in nearly all languages the word denoting it is feminine.

The interventions of the Virgin thus far considered concern material life. There are others, doubtless much more important, where Mary as warrior fights against spiritual enemies. She is then the 'Chastisement of invisible enemies', 'Destruction of demons', 'She who has overthrown the empire of the tyrant of men'. The foundation and justification of this role are obviously found in the well-known passage of Genesis (3:14), where God says to the serpent, 'I will put enmity between you and the woman, etc.' Hence prayers like the following, taken from Latin euchology:

August Queen of the heavens and Mistress of the Angels, you who received from God the power and the mission to crush the head of Satan, humbly we beseech you, send your holy legions, that by your orders and through your power, they might pursue the demons, engaging them everywhere and quelling their audacity, and drive them back into the abyss.

The reference to 'holy legions' explains why St Michael the Archangel, who is known as the Arch-strategist, is often associated with the cult of the Virgin at Marian sanctuaries like Mont-Saint-Michel, Rocamadour and Le Puy.

Fearless warrior, Mary is nevertheless also—and it is in this role that she is best known—*Virgo clemens* and *Mater misericordiae*, the

Mother full of love for her children and full of solicitude in their sorrows. 'I am the Mother of noble love,' she declares on several occasions in the liturgy. We have already seen her provide help to sailors. She is also *Salus infirmorum*, 'Health of the sick': there are hundreds of books telling of cures by Mary, cures of the deaf, dumb and blind, paralytics, epileptics, etc., and of raisings of the dead. Let us recall the *Livre des miracles de Notre-Dame de Chartres* (The Book of Miracles of Our Lady of Chartres) by Jehan Marchant; the *Livre des miracles de Notre-Dame de Rocamadour*, dating from 1172, which mentions 90 cures, including that of madmen; the record edited by the Benedictines of Toulouse concerning cures by the Black Virgin of la Daurade; and without going back so far, we need only think of Lourdes. Mary is also 'merciful' as *Consolatrix afflic-torum*, 'Consolation of the afflicted', and above all as *Refugium pec-catorum*, 'Refuge of sinners': it is particularly with regard to them that she appears as 'Mother of mercy'. At present we shall not dwell on this point, for we plan to examine it in greater detail later; at this juncture we shall merely note the relationship between Mary the merciful and the dead. Rather curiously a certain number of her statues were found in necropoles, like the Virgin of Arles, which came from the cemetery of Alyscamps, that of Coulandon, from a Gallo-Roman necropolis and that at Manosque, found in a sar-cophagus. Others are associated with a necropolis: the abbey of St Victor at Marseilles for instance is built over one; the Black Virgin of Mauriac is adjacent to an important third century cemetery; Our Lady of Riom bears the title 'Notre-Dame du Marthuret', the same word as *martrois*, the mediaeval name for an old cemetery and there is also, as we saw earlier, an ancient cemetery at Mont-Saint-Michel, whence the name Mont-Tombe. What emerges from these observa-tions is, first, the obvious connection with the *earth*; then the pro-tective role of the Virgin over the dead, that is, over their destiny in the Beyond; we shall need to speak again of this also.

In our opinion, this just completed survey of all the titles, names, and symbols of the Virgin found in the mass of canonical prayers or, at least, prayers accepted by the liturgy—we emphasize this point—constitutes a truly impressive whole that forces us to make the following inescapable observation, namely, that these names, titles and symbols hardly belong to an ordinary woman, above all when we note that several of the titles, such as 'Queen of the world' and 'Queen of Heaven', also belong to Christ, who, in a strictly symmetrical way, is called 'King of the world' and 'King of Heaven'. This parallel, moreover, poses a delicate problem which we shall not examine at present, but to which we shall return when we have at hand the appropriate means of explanation. What will engage us now is another parallel, that of the majority of these Marian names, titles and symbols to those of the pre-Christian divinities we encountered in the first chapter. As we shall see, this parallel is altogether illuminating and explains in depth how the cult of Mary could validly replace that of the pre-Christian goddesses, for, under such circumstances, this is not the perception of vague similarities, but of altogether prime elements.

Upon consideration, the phenomenon is easily explained, given that here we are dealing with not only a universal sacred reality, but one which for thousands of years imbued and, so to say, shaped the soul and religious feelings of a whole segment of mankind. All the divine beings we have met with issue from the Great Mother, the *Magna Mater*, in whom the principle of all life resides, who appeared for our sake—and I mean precisely this—at the end of the Neolithic age in the Europe of dolmens and covered dolmenic walkways, in all of the Mediterranean Basin, the Near East, and into India, thus even before the invasion of Indo-Europeans, among whom, however, she continued to play a role of first importance. All goddess mothers descend from this archetype, from the Cretan and Anatolian Great Mothers, who were the source of the more recent forms we have known, Demeter, Cybele, Artemis, Ishtar and the Greco-Roman Isis, to the Celtic divine figures, Belisama, Ana, etc. While all have been enriched with new traits, in particular according to different times and places, all have nevertheless preserved the fundamental traits characteristic of this sacred type: they are first and foremost chthonic, that is, divinities of the earth, of water, fecundity, the fields, and vegetation, but at the same time have some of the characteristics of the whole cosmos, the stars, and the heavens, without being confused, we emphasize this, with the materiality of the elements of the world, at least before the age of their decline, because they possessed authentic divinity and therefore transcended the visible world. In addition, these divinities are 'mothers', and often 'spouses', but at the same time 'virgins', as Ch. Picard has clearly shown in his studies of the pre-Hellenic religions, conclusions that apply equally to all chthonic divinities; this apparent contradiction only serves to convey, by means of an oxymoron, the fact that the divine type in question is defined by its capacity, as 'earth', to receive every form from 'heaven' and be impregnated with it without ever being exhausted.

To start, let us consider Demeter (Ceres). Her chthonic character is too obvious to dwell on, as is the second trait she shares with all the other divinities under consideration, that of being at once 'virgin' and 'mother'. And we hardly need mention the obvious parallel with Mary on these two points. More interesting will be to pursue this parallel with regard to the particular traits of the goddess, her attributes, or the details of her cult: we shall find they include a good number of those seen to belong to the Virgin Mary.

Thus, because of her chthonic nature, Demeter was often associated with the *grotto*. Such was the case with the *black* Demeter of Phigalia, in the Peloponnese, some kilometres from the famous temple of Bassae. The wild, almost hostile, character of the site is striking: the gorge of the River Neda, opening at the foot of a high wall of Mount Elaion, forms a tunnel of churning water some hundred metres long, whence the name *Aspra Nera* ('White Waters'). The sacred grotto of the goddess is found in the high wall, about thirty-five meters above the water. The site recalls Rocamadour, where the sacred grotto also opens high up on the flank of the cliff dominating the valley. The similarity would have been even greater in the Middle Ages, when the sites had the reputation of being almost terrifying. At Phigalia, the Virgin has 'occupied' the domain of Demeter, not only the grotto, but all the territory, and the gorge of the Neda is now called 'Stomion tis Panaghias', that is to say 'The Gorge of the All-Holy (Virgin)'.

As a divinity of vegetation, Demeter was first represented as a *tree*. Her primary function, though, was to preside over agriculture, the *work of the fields, harvests,* and *vintages.* She also often carried an *ear of wheat,* and sometimes a wreath of wheat ears, in place of the usual *calathos*, which is a basket of fruit. This close connection with agriculture also explains why the color green is one of her attributes, and there was even a 'Green Demeter' (*Demeter Chlora*) not far from the Black. It also explains why the zodiacal *sign of the Virgin* with its large star, 'Spica', the 'Ear of Wheat', was consecrated to her: the harvest season opens on 22 August, the date the sun enters this sign. Moreover, all Demeter's feasts were agricultural, and in her most famous cult, that of Eleusis, the two great ceremonies of initiation, those of the Lesser and Greater Mysteries, celebrated in February and September respectively, framed the cycle of the agricultural year. As chthonic power, Demeter was a *guardian and protectress of the dead*. Given these circumstances, we might be astonished that one of her attributes was sometimes the *dove*, for example at Phygalia, for the dove is a symbol of spiritual ascension. Here, however, the presence of the dove can be explained in two ways: first, as the heritage of the Minoan Great Goddess, whose kinship with Demeter is well-known, and with whom the dove was a constant attribute, as can be seen on a host of statuettes and cult objects found in Crete at Mycenae and Tirynth; a second reason, which may be surprising at first, is that this bird is the symbol of initiation, at which, precisely, the goddess presided, especially at Eleusis. Let us recall at this juncture that in the Greek Church we encounter *chalices* decorated with a dove.

Like Demeter, *Cybele* was a divinity of vegetation associated with a *tree*, in this case the pine. She was likewise consecrated to the color *green* and a frequenter of *grottoes*. Let us note in this regard that the grotto has featured in the cult of all chthonic divinities, since remotest Antiquity, as is witnessed by those dedicated to the Minoan Great Mother, such as the famous one of Psychro, on Crete. In the same way the oldest sanctuary of the Anatolian great goddess, near Heracleia Pontica, was a grotto. And what is of particular interest to our subject is the fact that the ritual grotto was widespread throughout Western Europe and Gaul; in the first chapter, we had occasion to mention the many remaining traces of it. As already stated, the grotto is a symbol of the world: it is especially a place where vital forces concentrate, whence its association with the phenomenon of birth, the product of such a concentration, whether it concern the physical birth of a child or spiritual birth or rebirth, which explains the role so often played by grottoes in the performance of initiatic rites. If we dwell somewhat upon this subject, it is because the grotto occupies, as we have already seen, a place of prime importance in the Marian cult, not only in connection with the Virgin's presence in such a place at Christ's Nativity, but also with regard to many holy places, like Lourdes, and to sanctuaries where crypts, especially those of Black Virgins, substitute for grottoes.

We have just cited Lourdes, where we have an example of the frequent association of springs with the Marian grotto. This was also the case in the cult of Cybele, who was more particularly a water divinity, presiding over fountains and springs, and especially thermal springs. Here we have another special characteristic of divinities of fecundity and of the Great Mother. In India, the *Maha Devi* is even said to have been born in water. This explains the well-known rite of bathing the statues of these divinities, a rite that is known to be celebrated annually for the statues of the Saints Mary of the Sea. What is less known, is that in several regions of France, in cases of drought, statues of the Holy Virgin were bathed in the same way, right up until the nineteenth century.

Fertility is also the work of the *moon*, a nearly constant attribute of the Great Mother; Cybele, too, wore a *crescent*. This is also why her chariot, which iconographically is usually drawn by lions, was, in certain processions, drawn by oxen, which refers us to the symbolism of the *bull*. Concerning this, let us note certain vestigial customs: at Barjols (Var) where there is a Black Virgin, a traditional bull dance is performed at the start of spring, while at Mèze (Languedoc) the bull festival takes place—not by chance—on 15 August!

Here now are some titles that curiously recall, some word for word, those of the Virgin Mary: *Queen of Earth, Queen of Heaven, Lady of the Sea, Helpful to Men.* The last virtue was concerned with several activities, including the *protection of cities*—Cybele too was occasionally represented as castellated—and the *protection of the dead,* but also a spiritual role which reveals an unexpected aspect of her cult during the imperial epoch; she was called *guardian of souls against the spirit of evil.*

We cannot fail to mention *Maia*, another divinity of vegetation, for she certainly gave her name to the month of *May*. At the close of Antiquity and in the first centuries of our era, the Roman Maia, whose name signifies 'mother', and the Greek Maia, mother of Hermes, fused to form a single divine entity honored at various places throughout the Empire and whose feast was celebrated on 15 *May*. Some have wished to relate the name *Maia* to *Maria*, which would be quite legitimate within the order of symbolic etymology.

Like Demeter and Cybele, *Artemis* (Diana), especially Artemis of Ephesus, was, a hypostasis of the Great Mother, both *virgin* and *fecund*, and *Mother of the gods*. By this very fact, she, to, was linked to *agriculture* and *animal husbandry* and in many places was also associated with the *bull*, bearing the title *Tauropolos* in Altic and Phocaea, while in Arcadia she was for the same reason connected with the *moon*. Like the other hypostases of the Great Mother, one of her primary symbols was the *tree*, and this should be emphasized a little, for, regarding the Ephesian Artemis, who is 'Asiatic', the sacred tree is a widely distributed motif, found throughout the Near East, in Assur, Egypt, Anatolia, etc., and also in Crete. The tree was seen as an epiphany of the fertility divinity, and thus we have the Minoan goddess seated on a ring of gold near the Tree of Life, found at Mycenae; often the divinity was even fused with the tree, as with the Egyptian Isis-Hathor forming part of a sycamore, the celestial Tree of Immortality, and dispensing refreshments to the deceased, a scene found in an engraving from the *Sargophagus Texts* (see Plate V [1]). Earlier, we saw that the Black Virgin of Foggia is presented in a very similar way (Plate V [2]). This is a constant theme in the history of religions. Artemis was assimilated to a tree, at both Karyai, in Laconia, and Orchomene, in Arcadia, where she appeared as *Kedreatis*, that is to say, Artemis-cedar. Now the Artemis of Ephesus was associated with the *vine*, and this, again, is very significant: the vine was considered the vegetal expression of immortality, especially in the Near East, and was very often consecrated to the Great Mother. The Tammuz cycle includes a goddess, sister of the god, with the name 'Celestial Vine'; in Anatolia the vine, consecrated to the Great Mother, who is closely connected with Artemis of Ephesus, was designated 'Tree of life' and 'Staff of life'.

Here, also, we find ourselves very close to Mary who, as we have seen, was assimilated to the 'true Vine bearing the fruit of life'.

But more importantly, as 'Queen of the night', a title linked from the start to the lunar symbol, the Ephesian Artemis also bore the title *Queen of heaven*. And the *litanies* of her daily cult enumerated all her virtues and titles of glory; she was honored as *she who heals* (*alexikakos*), *she who protects sailors* (she was therefore *stella maris*), and *she who protects the dead*. Once again we find ourselves on familiar ground.

From this we understand how easy it was, after the Council of Ephesus, for the Christians of that city to pass, so to speak, from one cult to the other, especially as the memories of Mary's last years, spent just outside Ephesus, remained very much alive. As Ch. Picard pointed out in an article in the 1938 *Eranos*, at Ephesus Mary became a hypostasis of Artemis Parthenos, Virgin Artemis. Her tomb was set on the slopes of the Solmissos, the goal of 'pagan' pilgrimages and site of the oribatids, that is, the processions of Artemis across the mountain. Her house is also there, together with the *grotto* to which she used to withdraw, and the chapel of the 'Virgin of the Plane-trees.' In his book *La sculpture antique*, Picard wrote: 'A feminine cult was not only found to have been substituted at Ephesus itself, for the ancient suzerainty of Artemis, but in this rival cult the aspect of the divine mother continued to be determined by the past; Artemis Parthenos was encountered once again in Mary's traits'; and he notes that in the first centuries of our era statues of Artemis of Ephesus were often classed together with those of Mary.

In order to forestall certain objections, let us make it clear that the presence of Mary at Ephesus at the end of her life was established definitively by the mixed religious and archeological commission of 1892, which confirmed the still-living local oral tradition. The other tradition, according to which she ended her life in Jerusalem, a tradition still held by the Byzantine Church, came later and is without serious foundation. *From this, how can we not see in the circumstances that led St John the Apostle to take Mary to Ephesus to end her earthly life a barely veiled intention of Divine Providence?*

Given the extraordinary influence her cult exercised throughout the Empire, we should also pay particular attention to *Isis*. Let us immediately specify that we have in mind the Gallo-Roman Isis, who was somewhat different from the purely Egyptian goddess, to the extent that, while keeping her original traits, she became a form of the *Magna Mater*. From this commanding position she integrated the general characteristics and absorbed other divine personalities that had issued from her. This was particularly the case with *Ishtar* (or Astarte), the Aphrodite (Venus) of Sumer and Canaan, which should not be forgotten, for, as we are about to observe, both she and Isis are a sure source of the titles and attributes encountered in the cult of the Virgin Mary, as can be judged by the impressive number of parallels we have turned up.

As concerns Isis, they are drawn from the *litanies* transmitted by Apuleus in book XI of the *Golden Ass*, the *Hymn of Isidoros* found at Medinet Maadi, the *Hymns of Kyme* and *Philae*, and finally Diodorus of Sicily (1, 25).

The image conveyed to us by Isis is certainly that of the Great Mother with all her attributes. As *Celestial Ceres, Mother of all nature, Mistress of all the elements*, she is the great life force, whence her representation as the heavenly *cow*. She is the *Great in Heaven, Mistress of constellations* (which corresponds to *Regina coeli*) and 'sits in the splendor of the sun'; she is *All-powerful* (*omnipotens* in Latin, which corresponds to the title *Virgo potens* given to Mary); she is *Queen of the gods* (which corresponds to Mary's title, *Queen of the angels*, a title needing further explanation), and *Queen of the Manes*, that is, the Dead. Her activity is characterized by kindness and goodwill; she is the *Perpetual salvation of mankind*, she *saves cities from war* and *heals the sick* (reminiscent of *salus infirmorum*); she preserves *those who sail on the great sea*, and is thus *stella maris*; she is called *Isis Pelagia*, that is to say 'Marine Isis', an important title that refers to the tradition ascribing the invention of navigation to her, a tradition originally from Alexandria, where, according to Juvenal, she had a temple full of ex-votos. At the start of the sailing season she was offered the first ship launched on the sea (Apuleus XI, 17). Given the influence it had on the cult of Mary and especially of the Black Virgin, we draw attention to this aspect of the cult of Isis, and are reminded of the legend concerning the origin of Our Lady of Boulogne and of the little boats of Our Lady of Confession at Marseilles. Finally, to end this list of Isis' titles and virtues, let us remember that she is *the merciful* (which refers us to *mater misericordiae*) and, as such, *has enjoined compassion for supplicants.*

The titles of *Ishtar-Venus* both match and complete those of Isis. She is *virgin* and at the same time *spouse of the gods* (Mary is called *spouse of God* in the Acathist litanies). As goddess of fecundity, Ishtar-Venus is called *source* and *giver of life* (we have also seen Mary called *zoodotis*), and is associated with the *moon* and, lastly, called *saving cow.* Like Cybele she is a *warrior* and it should be noted with regard to this that the trait of warrior is often attributed to 'virgins': thus Athena (Minerva) who, as we know, is *Wisdom,* is also called the *unconquerable* and the *terror of enemies* (an expression we have seen applied to Mary too); likewise, in India, Kali is called *Durga,* 'the Terrible'.

We know from the Bible (Jer. 7:18; 44:17–19) that in Canaan, Ishtar-Venus bore the title *Queen of Heaven* (*Regina coeli*); she was also *Mother of mercy, She who listens to prayer* and *She who intercedes with angered gods.* Like Isis and Artemis, she was *protectress of mariners* and bore the title *Star of the sea* (*stella maris*), whence the two symbols of the *dove* and the *rose.*

It should not be surprising that we speak of Aphrodite and the Virgin Mary in the same breath, for the Aphrodite we have in mind is the *Aphrodite Ourania,* the *Venus coelestis,* who presides over pure love; and this explains how symbols like the dove and the rose can belong to both Aphrodite and Mary, who presents herself as the 'Mother of Noble Love' in the epistle for the Vigil of 8 December, taken from *Ecclesiastes* (24:23–31).

At any rate it is easy to understand that the titles, symbols, and invocations of Ishtar-Aphrodite, like those of Isis, Artemis, Cybele, and Demeter, should pass into the Marian liturgy, it having been compiled initially in the Near East, in the territories of these divine entities.

We are far from having such rich and exact documentation on the Celtic and Gaelic forms of the Great Mother, whose influence, as we have seen, was of prime importance in the evolution of the Marian cult. Nevertheless, the little we do know leads us to think that they were described and invoked in a similar fashion, since we learn, for example, that *Belisama* was considered a *warrior* and called *Victory*, while in the form of *Brigantia*, she was a *healer*, and, as *Epona*, was *protectress of the dead*, and that, during the period that concerns us, these different hypostases had absorbed parallel Greco-Roman divinities from whom they would have taken over titles and attributes.

It seems that, having come to the end of our inquiry into the epicleses and titles of the Virgin Mary and collated them with those of pre-Christian divine forms, we are now in a position to answer the question posed at the end of the first chapter, namely, are we not compelled to state that Mary can be considered a 'divine personality?' Now all the evidence would suggest an affirmative response. Doubtless it will be objected that the ecclesiastical magisterium has always rejected such a conclusion. This is true, but we nevertheless notice three things. The first, already mentioned, is that the invocations to the Virgin and the titles we have examined, all of which are canonically permitted by the Church, are not reasonably suited to an ordinary woman. The second is that the Christian people, obeying a sort of fundamental religious instinct, have always tended to conduct themselves vis-à-vis Mary *as though* she belonged to the supra-human world, or the divine order. As proof of this we offer the attitude of Villon in the 'Ballad to Our Lady', in which he has his mother, without hesitation, call Mary 'High Goddess'. Just a literary formula, or poetic hyperbole, it will be said. Perhaps, but the characteristic of poets is often, precisely, to express the profound but sometimes obscure intuitions and convictions of a people. And I am not aware that Villon felt uneasy about this remark, and this at a time when one did not trifle with such matters; when he did feel uneasy, it was for his mischievous pranks. Thirdly and finally, we find in the prayers and also in the writings of the most orthodox spiritual authors, the two titles 'Divine Mother' and 'Divine Mary', both of which are amply justified by the title 'Mother of God' or Theotokos, conferred by the Council of Ephesus, a title whose meaning seems not to have been exhausted by the current official theological explanation, as already noted.

Whether we like it or not, the question thus arises, and cannot be avoided. To our way of thinking, the only way to deal with it is to situate it within an accurate view of the relationships between the two great religious forms of monotheism and polytheism. From the point of view of believers, these relationships have always been, and continue to be, envisaged in a spirit of radical exclusiveness. Such a spirit is no doubt explained and justified up to a certain point by the fact that if a given religious form is to maintain its specificity, it is obliged to practice a certain exclusiveness with regard to other forms; and we should add the far from negligible reason that the whole problem of polytheism in Christian lands has been dominated, even to the present day, by a criticism of Greco-Roman polytheism. This criticism is justified to the extent that the latter was in many respects decadent and in its final phase, and had sunk into naturalism and idolatry—except, however, that some spheres of this polytheism and, in particular, that of the cults we are dealing with had, as already mentioned, re-discovered certain authentic sacred values, and that, in any case, the symbols they incarnated obviously retained their truth and so could be revived at any moment. That said, it is undeniable that, as a whole, this polytheism merited the pejorative term 'paganism'. But it is very far from being the case that polytheism in itself is paganism, which is but the degraded form of the former. The current attitude of the Catholic Church in this area has been considerably modified; developments in the history of religions have shown that there are polytheisms of an incontestable religious value, and the most demanding monotheist can no longer claim that Hinduism, for example, is pagan in the same way as the religions of classical Antiquity's decline. The Catholic Church allows that the great religions possess 'truth in a partial manner', to use the official canonical expression, an expression we need not comment on here.

All that is required, therefore, is a simple return to the natural fundamental definitions of monotheism and polytheism. These two religious forms correspond to two aspects of the Divinity: transcendence and immanence. In relation to His creation, the total universe, God is simultaneously transcendent and immanent; transcendent in His Essence, that is to say, radically other than the universe and the beings filling it, and immanent through His power and activity, because the universe only subsists through the divine power that is in it and keeps it in existence. For a particular reason, the emphasis can be placed more strongly upon transcendence, thereby establishing a radical separation between God and the universe, and this is the monotheistic position. Or, for a different reason, emphasis can be placed on immanence, without, however, any denial of transcendence—failing which, there is a fall into idolatry and naturalism. In the monotheistic perspective, divinity belongs to God alone, the Unique, and all beings are simply creatures; in the polytheistic perspective, there is certainly the acknowledgement of the Divine Unity, the supreme Divinity, which by definition can only be unique, but there is recognition that, by way of the creative act itself, the different classes of beings receive something from Divinity and possess in themselves, as a reflection of their source, something that is more or less divine. From another point of view, a distinction is made in God between the Divine Essence and the Divine Qualities, also called Divine Attributes or Names, which are 'aspects' of the Divinity, but not its supreme Aseity. Starting from here, polytheism admits that these Divine Attributes can be hypostasized, and they are then presented as 'gods'; these are the 'great gods' that 'surround' the Supreme God. On the other hand, beings that reflect these Attributes or Divine Qualities to a high degree are also called 'gods', but occupy a rank that is obviously inferior to the 'great gods.' They correspond to the 'angels' of monotheism.

We thus see that there are not several equal 'Gods'—with a capital letter—in polytheism, as is popularly thought, which, besides, is contradictory in its very conception. These 'gods'—with a small letter—in no wise compromise, if one may so express it, the unicity and transcendence of the supreme God.

Having thus clearly defined things, it seems that monotheism and polytheism can be regarded, apart from their use in worship, as two 'languages' applying to the same realities, but seen from different—complementary rather than contradictory—points of view. This being the case, a given religious reality should be able to express itself in either of the two languages; a reality taught in a monotheistic mode should be able to be translated into a polytheistic mode. In effecting the transposition, no change will be made to anything essential of the reality taught; on the contrary, it can gain by this, for polytheistic language allows light to be shed on certain aspects that the other language is inclined to veil somewhat, given the necessities inherent in it.

We touch here upon a point of particular interest to our subject. It is certainly a fact that Christian monotheism is hard pressed to adequately define the status of the Virgin Mary in all its ramifications. We have proof of this in the word *hyperdulia*, chosen by the Church to denote the type of worship that should be accorded her. *Dulia* (Greek *doulia*) is the worship authorized for saints and means 'veneration', as opposed to *latria*, the worship reserved for God, which is 'adoration'. The *hyperdulia* reserved for the Virgin incontestably places her apart from and above the saints. This is all that is allowed by the monotheistic point of view, but it is definitely felt to be not altogether satisfactory, if only because it does not harmonize well with everything that the most official liturgy says of Mary, as we have amply shown, and as appears, moreover, in this hymn of Cosmas of Mayum, sung in the very middle of the anaphora, the most sacred part of the Byzantine Liturgy of St John Chrysostom:

> It is truly meet to bless Thee, O Theotokos, who art ever blessed and all pure, and Mother of our God. More honorable than the Cherubim, and incomparably more glorious than the Seraphim, who without stain didst bear God the Word, and art truly the Mother of God, Thee we magnify.

Finally, let us remember that, according to St Gregory Palamas, in his homily on the Annunciation, the Virgin 'alone is the boundary between created and uncreated natures.'

We are thus permitted to 'translate' the status of Mary into polytheistic language and, as a working hypothesis, consider her a *divine personality*, by remarking that the figure of the Virgin as we have seen it take shape during the study of her cult, is in a way the 'refraction' in a monotheistic environment, of the figure of the *Magna Mater* from ancient polytheism.

Let us expressly remark that this is not simply an intellectual game. The 'transposition' spoken of is made in our days: we have a thoroughly contemporary example of it in India. A recent report from a Catholic Missionary in Goa states that, without giving it a second thought, the Hindus have placed the Virgin Mary among their goddesses. What is more, this contemporary fact indicates what in all probability happened in the West during the first centuries of the Christian era.

Through our working hypothesis we shall be able to see that the Virgin Mary recapitulates and restores the ancient figure of the neolithic Great Mother, which, over the course of time, had deteriorated in some of its materialized forms since this divine power was often linked solely to cosmic elements, but nevertheless preserved the initial great truth through the support of traditional sacred symbols. The spiritual message that the pre-Christian figures were no longer able to deliver passed over to Mary, in whom the total truth burned anew through the eternal symbols she salvaged, a truth that is, as we shall see, an essential element of every religious conception.

3

The Mother of God

UP TO THIS POINT we have examined the circumstances and external signs that have contributed to the formation of the figure and cult of Mary as successor to the various earlier representations of the *Magna Mater*. In doing so we have exhausted the historical aspect of the problem—at least in its essential elements, for volumes could be written on the subject—and done what could be called a 'horizontal' exegesis. We need now to proceed to a 'vertical' exegesis, to consider the subject according to the vertical axis of the cross, the cross being, here as elsewhere, the fundamental frame of reference, that is to say, to re-ascend to the ontological principle incarnate in the type of the Great Mother, and consequently, according to our hypothesis, in the Virgin Mary.

If the latter has a 'divine' character—recall that she is called 'Divine Mary' and 'Divine Mother'—the reason should not first be sought in the descent of the Holy Spirit upon her with a view to the incarnation of Christ, nor in her 'post mortem' glorification. On the contrary, these events are, in the case of the first, the consequence and, in the case of the second, proof of that exceptional state of sanctity which in a certain way can be regarded as 'divine.' What needs to be considered is something in the very person of Mary from her earthly birth; better still, one should look up-stream, so to speak, to before her birth. We immediately think of the privilege of the Immaculate Conception, which, in fact, is where the heart of the matter really lies. However, as indicated in the introduction, the Immaculate Conception is of such an extraordinary and transcendent nature that it cannot be explained and analyzed directly. We should first pinpoint the approaches to it found, as usual, in the treasures hidden in liturgical literature.

Now, on this subject, the liturgical literature offers us a theme for almost endless reflection. We have in mind two extracts from Scripture, one from *Ecclesiasticus* and the other from *Proverbs*, which, moreover, confirm each other perfectly. The first, which provides the 'capitulum' (short reading) for Vespers of the common of the Virgin, is expressed as follows: 'From the beginning was I created, and before all the worlds, and in the ages to come I shall not cease to be, and in the holy house I have exercised my ministry before him (the Lord)' (Eccl. 24:4). In the Bible, it is Wisdom personified who speaks thus, but here it is Mary, assimilated to Wisdom. The second text serves as the epistle for the Mass of the Feast of the Nativity of Our Lady on 8 September; it is still Wisdom, and therefore Mary, who speaks:

> The Lord possessed me in the beginning of his ways, before he made anything from the beginning. I was set up from eternity, and of old before the earth was made. The depths were not as yet, and I was already conceived, neither had the fountains of waters as yet sprung out. The mountains with their huge bulk had not as yet been established: before the hills I was brought forth. He had not yet made the earth, nor the rivers, nor the poles of the world. When he prepared the heavens, I was present. When with a certain law and compass he enclosed the depths, when he established the sky above, and poised the fountains of waters, when he compassed the sea with its bounds, and set a law to the waters that they should not pass their limits, when be balanced the foundations of the earth; I was with him forming all things, and was delighted every day, playing before him at all times, playing in the world. . . . (Prov. 8:22–31)

This text is better known than the first, but it seems highly probable that very few people have any real idea of its deeper meaning and implications. Too often it is seen simply as a poetic elaboration that need not be taken literally, whereas it is in fact nothing less than a simultaneously luminous and veiled testimony to the eternal birth of the Virgin in the 'region' of the Divinity. More particularly, the liturgy invites us to view things this way by giving us this Scriptural passage for meditation precisely on 8 September, the Feast of the

Nativity of Mary, suggesting that we pass from the consideration of her earthly, temporal birth to that of her heavenly, eternal birth.

The somewhat complex concept of 'Wisdom' will be elucidated later. What needs to be remembered for the moment is the presence of a feminine being, under the name of Wisdom, associated somewhat mysteriously with God the creator. This might initially astonish those accustomed to the way God is presented in Judaeo-Christian monotheism. However, the presence of the 'Feminine' in God is not only affirmed by Scripture, but is also a metaphysical axiom. The Scriptural affirmation is well-known, and can be found at the beginning of Genesis (1:27) in the account of the creation of man: 'So God created man in his image, in the image of God created he him; male and female created he them'; whence follows a necessary conclusion, namely that if the masculine-feminine polarity constitutes the image of God in man, it is because this polarity in some way exists in God. And it is a metaphysical axiom because a thing existing in creation must necessarily have its prototype in the Creator, failing which it would not exist.

The difficulty in accepting this truth stems largely from the fact that the polarity is considered uniquely from the point of view of the sexes, as of 'male and female', whereas it refers in the first place to the genders, 'masculine and feminine', which have a very different import. There is an essential difference here, which it is important to keep in mind in order to avoid a host of erroneous opinions. Sex, in fact, is nothing but an adaptation to organic life of a polarity governing the whole of creation; it is but one of the things constituting the masculine or feminine genders, which in their turn, apply to levels of existence where sexual polarity has no role, except in a symbolic sense. Put differently, and contrary to current opinion, 'masculine' and 'feminine' are not notions derived from 'male' and 'female'. Quite the opposite; it is the latter that are but aspects of the masculine and feminine genders. In reality, masculine and feminine are discernible at every degree of the created order: for example in the pairs 'heaven-earth', 'sun-moon', 'day-night', 'solid-liquid', 'fire-water', 'dry-moist', 'gold-silver', 'sulphur-mercury', etc. These are some of the qualities manifesting, each in its way, the universal polarity governing the whole of cosmic life, a polarity that the tradition of the Far East calls *yang* and *yin*, or the active and passive aspects of the Universal Energy, and which is rooted in God Himself. God is not only, or firstly, 'masculine'; 'masculine' and 'feminine' are indispensable revelations, or 'prolongations', to use Frithjof Schuon's expression, of the Divine Source, the Supreme Divinity being at once the one and the other, with the relation between them manifesting the mystery of divine life, the divine Bi-unity, in the visible world. Thus woman is mother, therefore creatrix, and the Divinity can also be conceived under feminine form; St Thomas Aquinas himself said somewhere that God is simultaneously Father and Mother.

We need to examine this mystery of divine life in relation to creation, for herein lies the Marian Mystery, as is suggested by the Epistle for the Feast of 8 September.

This examination should be conducted according to metaphysical doctrine, and in order to do so, we shall make use of the formulation of the latter found in the Hindu tradition. It is not that the elements of this doctrine, which, after all is universal, cannot be found in Plato or Denis the Areopagite, for example, but its Hindu formulation attains a degree of precision not to be found elsewhere, both in each of the terms employed and in the combination of concepts, thereby providing us with a frame of reference.

The point to start from is the distinction between the Absolute and the Relative, the Supreme, Divine Reality and Universal Relativity, or again, the Principle and Manifestation, or Creation. The Supreme Reality, called *Atma* or *Parabrahma* in India, is the Beyond Being, the 'Super-Essential Thearchy' of Denis the Areopagite, absolutely unconditioned and unmanifested, the two aspects of which are the Absolute and the Infinite. The Absolute, again, is the Essence, Transcendence, Beyond-Being properly so-called, the Godhead; and the Infinite is Universal Possibility or All-Possibility, Potentiality in itself, the potentiality of beings and things, Immanence. Within itself, the Absolute contains Masculinity itself, and the Infinite, Femininity itself. In parenthesis, let us note that we need to take great care lest these abstract terms deceive us, for they are abstract only in form and in relation to our minds, while in fact hiding the highest realities, for we are here at the supreme level whence everything derives.

From the Infinitude of Atma, the Supreme Principle, arises *Maya*, or Manifestation, which, at its summit, comprises the personal God, who is pure Being, the reflection of the Supreme Principle, God the Creator, Leglislator, and Savior, eternally 'born' of the Divine or Supreme Essence or Godhead, 'which is even beyond [the personal] God', and which 'engenders God', as Denis the Areopagite puts it (*Divine Names* 2:1,4). Before proceeding further, we should clarify the meaning of the word *Maya*, which, through often being mistranslated as 'illusion', has been a source of grave misunderstandings, leading to the assimilation of the Indian metaphysics to German Idealism, with which it is clearly in no way connected. In actual fact the word refers to the idea of 'art', and we are immediately aware here that it is a question of 'divine art', the source of Manifestation or Creation.

Moreover, two *Mayas* are to be distinguished: 'Supreme Maya', in the principial order, of which we have just spoken, and 'Lower Maya', in the cosmological order, and therefore below the personal creator God, and designating creation as a whole.

The arising of Universal Maya is brought about by the divine Energy of the Principle inherent in Infinitude; this Energy, which is another aspect of Maya, is called *Shakti*, of which, like Maya, there are also two: *Maha Shakti* within the Supreme Principle—this is All-Possibility containing Universal Maya, or the Energy which projects Relativity as Universal Maya—and Shakti at the level of Being, as its creative power.

Shakti is the *maternal aspect* of the Supreme Divinity, and is the 'other' in God, that is to say the universe, which is in Him as a 'passive unity', what is called the *Eternal Feminine*. This Femininity, this Shakti, is the cause of creation: without principial Femininity God would not be participable, there would be no creation; the Eternal Feminine contains the mystery of that 'divine epiphany' which is all of creation.

The Personal God, the first Being, called *Ishvara* in India, receives from the Mahashakti the possibilities of manifestable beings and conceives them in his Logos, or Word. At this stage, beings are so many modes of the divine essence; God knows them as *archetypes*, that is to say as images capable of participating in his essence, but at

Map according to E. Salliens, *Nos Vierges Noires*, showing
the distribution of black statues in France around 1550.

I

1. Isis Kourotrophos (nurturer of the young)
   holding the infant Horus. Greco-Roman era
   (Foquet collection).

2. Artemis, from the temple built by Croesus (sixth century BC).

3. Black Isis molded in black clay from the Nile. Under this form
   she symbolizes the fertile earth (Fouquet collection).
   Origin: lower Egypt.

II

Virgin with Child
Fresco from the catacomb of Priscilla
(second century AD).

III

Adoration of the Magi; silver reliquary
(fourth century AD) from the church of
St Nazarius Major, Milan

IV

1.   2.

1.
Hathor-Isis giving food and drink, from her tree,
to the deceased (after a monument in the Berlin Museum).

2.
The Black Virgin of Foggia (Italy).
Objects associated with the legend are to be seen
around the tree: the ox, the plowman, the guiding light.

Statuette of a Gallo-Roman mother goddess
from Prunay-le-Gillon (Eure-et-Loire).
Musée Ant. Nat.

1.

2.

Gallo-Roman mother goddesses:

1.
Statue from the Musée de Saintes

2.
Statue discovered at the bottom of a funerary
pit near Bernard (Vendée, second century AD).
The child was accidentally broken off.

VII

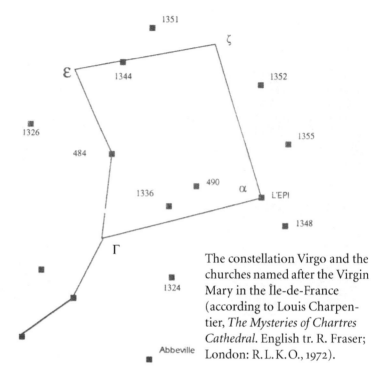

The constellation Virgo and the churches named after the Virgin Mary in the Île-de-France (according to Louis Charpentier, *The Mysteries of Chartres Cathedral*. English tr. R. Fraser; London: R.L.K.O., 1972).

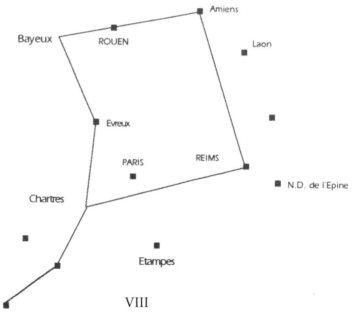

VIII

The Black Virgin of Rocamadour (twelfth century).

The Black Virgin of Marsat (Puy-de-Dôme, twelfth century).

X

The Black Virgin of Meymac (Corrèze, twelfth century).

The former statue of Notre Dame de Puy sketched by Foujas,
from Saint-Fond in 1778 and burned by the revolutionaries.

XII

Restoration, by Besset, of the former statue
of Puy according to the documents of Foujas.

XIII

The present day Black Virgin in the basilica at Puy.

The former statue at Chartres after a
seventeenth century etching (Cabinet des Estampes).

XV

Chartres, present day statue of Our Lady Under-the-Earth

Our Lady of Good Hope (Dijon, twelfth century)
represented as pregnant. The entire lower portion has deteriorated.

XVII

The strangest and perhaps the most mysterious of the
Black Virgins: Notre Dame de Belloch, at Dorres
(Pyrénées Orientale, eleventh century).

XVIII

Our Lady of Confession, the Black Virgin of Marseille
(Abbey of St Victor, thirteenth century).

XIX

Our Lady of Good Deliverance,
a Paris Black Virgin now at Neuilly-sur-Seine.

XX

Notre Dame de Thuret (Puy-de-Dôme)

XXI

Our Lady of the Snows (Aurillac)

XXII

Our Lady of the Castle (Saint-Christophe, Cantal)

XXIII

Notre Dame de Romigier (Manosque)

XXIV

The Black Virgin of the Mende cathedral
(twelfth–thirteenth century)

Our Lady of the Ramparts (Eglise du Tour, Toulouse)

XXVI

Notre Dame de Hal (Belgium)

XXVII

The Black Virgin of Monserrat (Spain)

XXVIII

The Black Virgin of the Benedictine Abbey
of Einsiedeln (Switzerland)

XXIX

The Virgin of Maria Bistrica
(Zagreb region, Croatia)
Plate from the Croatian Catholic Mission

Our Lady of Czestochova (Poland)

XXXI

Our Lady of Kazan (Russia)

XXXII

this level, the archetypes are God Himself and there is no 'other', and therefore no creation. For the latter to be realized, the activity of the Logos needs to be exercised on an 'other'; Ishvara is polarized into *Purusha* and *Prakriti*; *Purusha* is his creative essence, and *Prakriti*— the necessary otherness which is *Materia prima*, that mysterious, ungraspable, abyssal entity—is pure and universal Passivity, the universal Substrate; not 'nothing' in itself, it is without form while receiving all forms; pure Receptivity, cosmic Receptacle, it is that which being 'other' than the divine Essence enables the archetypes to manifest themselves. In relation to the creative divine Essence it is universal Substance; the creative Essence projects the archetypes onto it, and it is thereby made fertile, and becomes *Prakriti*, or Nature, *Natura naturans*; this is still Nature at the principial level, unmanifested in the visible, and to be distinguished from the lower *Prakriti*, which is effectuated Nature. This Nature, *Prakriti*, is also *Shakti* insofar as it has received the creative energy in itself, *passive* in relation to *Purusha*, the active pole of creation, it itself becomes *active* in relation to the world, to the archetypal beings that it projects into Existence; from power it becomes act; as *Shakti*, it is permanent activity, the source of life at every level; it is *Mother, Mother Nature, Magna Mater, Materia-Mater*. As such, in the polytheistic perspective, it is the consort of the creator. But since it always remains a fundamentally passive Power—formless yet containing forms—it is always 'virgin', 'immaculate', and entirely at the disposal of creative activity, its 'humble servant'.

Once again, this is a mysterious entity we are dealing with: at base, this Femininity, this 'passive unity', is 'pure nothingness'; but, for God, this 'naught' is eternally hidden by the image of absolute perfection received from Him. God sees His 'other' in principial Nature, an 'other' presenting to Him the image of a perfect woman. As Vladimir Soloviev says, the eternal Feminine is

> a living spiritual being, possessing the fullness of powers, a non-hypostatic being, but in search of hypostasis and aspiring to be indefinitely realized: the cosmic process is the realization of this Substance in a great number of forms and degrees.

It is also *Maya*, the reflection at the degree of Being of the Maya of the Supreme Principle mentioned earlier. It is the reflection of the Omnipotence of the Principle in the potentiality of *Materia prima*. It is Nature as product of 'Divine Art', since such is the exact meaning of Maya; still under this aspect, its activity is sometimes conceived as a 'game', the 'divine play', *lila*, an idea immediately reminiscent of the text from *Proverbs*, where Wisdom appeared 'playing' ceaselessly before God. This is because *Prakriti*, under its diverse aspects as Shakti and as Maya, is also considered to be Wisdom, taken in a completely analogous sense to that of the Judaeo-Christian tradition, which also brings us back to the mystery of the Virgin Mary considered as Wisdom.

Sophia or *Wisdom*, 'Holy Wisdom', is, at the highest level, the content of divine thought, the undifferentiated ensemble of the eternal archetypes of Creation, the *logoi*, according to Maximus the Confessor; when they are projected into *Materia prima*, it too becomes Wisdom, reflected Wisdom, called 'Creaturely Wisdom', a rather inadequate term. 'Emanated Wisdom' would be better, since it is still situated at the principial level and does not become created Wisdom except in its manifestation at lower degrees. Fr Sergei Bulgakov has dealt very thoroughly and at length with the aspects of Wisdom in his work *The Lamb of God*. In sum, Wisdom is another name for *Materia prima* fecundated by the Logos, and is the same as *Shakti* and *Maya;* its particularity resides in the fact that it has to do more with a certain aspect of creation: its order, harmony, and beauty.

In this way then, if Mary is assimilated to *Wisdom*, we can say she is equally the *Shakti, Maya,* and *Materia prima.* And we shall now add, the *Shekhina*, which we have not mentioned because this concept, belonging to the Jewish tradition, is extremely complex and, we think, will become clearer in the light of what has been expounded according to the Hindu tradition. Having said that, it is nevertheless essential to speak of the Shekhina in connection with the Virgin, for this concept features prominently in the Marian Mystery.

The concept of the Shekhina cannot be defined by one simple term; traditional texts number its aspects at about sixty. What is important for us, however, is to record the names and titles of the

The Mother of God

Shekhina that, as we shall see, are akin to those of the Virgin Mary. The word itself is connected with the root *shkn*, meaning 'to reside', 'to inhabit', and one of the meanings included in it is that of 'presence': it denotes the presence of God in the created, which is why we say the Shekhina is the 'Glory' (*kabod*) of God, that is to say, the reflection of God in things. It is also called the *Matrona*, the *Superior Mother*, and the *Queen*, and here we find ourselves upon familiar ground. The purpose of these names is to shed light upon the fundamental nature of the Shekhina; according to traditional authors, it is the feminine principle that unites with the *King*, the masculine principle (*Purusha-Prakriti* comes to mind), to establish, or re-establish, cosmic order; it is an uncreated creative Substance that brings all beings to birth in itself, the divine Receptivity, the totally available, passive Perfection. The analogy with the Shakti is easily recognized. Finally, the Shekhina is identified with Wisdom (*Hokmah*).

And so we find ourselves led to that point where the different doctrines converge, all expressing in their own language the same metaphysical realities, the same great mystery of creation within which the Marian Mystery is rooted; and it will be interesting to observe how what we have already said concerning this mystery is authenticated, as it were, by the Jewish tradition, the tradition to which Mary belonged during her earthly life.

Now the legitimate question is: how can Mary, an earthly woman before ascending to heaven, be called Wisdom, the Shekhina, or Shakti, Maya, and *Materia prima*. The answer is to be found in the notion of the *avatara*. This Hindu term is usually considered to mean 'incarnation', and more precisely a 'divine incarnation'. Its exact meaning, however, is (divine) 'descent', and it is used to designate 'divine descents' into the world that are not necessarily 'incarnations', as the word is understood in Christianity when speaking of the coming to earth of Christ. Christ was certainly an *avatara*, but constituted an incarnation in the strict sense, namely, a divine person united substantially to a human nature in such a way that He was definitively truly God and truly man, and this with a view to re-integrating man into the primordial state. The *avataras* encountered in the Hindu tradition are different and do not assume a similar importance; they are visible manifestations of the divine Principle in a human or sometimes animal form, without union of natures, and with the more limited mission of re-establishing the eternal Law, or *Dharma*, so as to put a stop to major disorders at certain critical moments in human history.

With this clarification we can say that Mary is an *avatara*, and she is presented as such by F. Schuon, for example, in his book *To Have a Center*. After listing the prerogatives granted to Mary by the Church, Schuon writes that

> a person possessing such prerogatives, to the point of being called 'Mother of God', necessarily has an avataric character, which, moreover, is expressed theologically by the Immaculate Conception.

And more precisely,

> Mary is a feminine *avatara* of the highest degree, which is proved by her rank as 'Spouse of the Holy Spirit' and 'Co-Redemptress'.

In Hindu terms one would say that the Virgin is an avatara of *Prakriti*, or *Materia prima*, or Universal Substance, or Universal Nature; and there should be nothing surprising about such an *avatara,* for *Prakriti*, as Shakti, is the principial prototype of Woman. Concerning this, Jean Borella, who has written superbly on the Marian Mystery in his book *La Charité profanée*, makes an essential point: he observes that the basis of the difference between Mary and ordinary women—and men—is the fact that her archetype is not, as with the others, in some way 'individual', so to speak, but on the contrary 'principial.' We might say that this is obvious, since *Prakriti*, as Universal Substance, is situated within the divine world. Let us specify, nevertheless, that this *avatara* is not an incarnation like that of Christ, which is impossible, since *Prakriti, Materia prima*, or Universal Substance is not an hypostasis or person, but a principle, and, as was said above, a spiritual organism or entity in search of hypostasis, but unable to be integrally hypostasized in a unique human person. Mary is a manifestation of Universal Substance, a perfect personification, which is to say that in her personal femininity the nature of Mary uniquely reflects divine principial Femininity, that is, absolute purity, and perfect virginity and maternity.

The avataric nature of the Virgin is expressed in an astonishingly accurate and precise way by her name, which has been interpreted in various ways. To some it had a reverential meaning, that of 'lady', while to St Jerome it meant *stella maris*, 'star of the sea', adopted liturgically in the hymn *Ave maris stella*. The most important meaning, however, is to be found at once hidden and revealed in the Hebrew written form. In Hebrew, the name is *Mariam;* this form was retained intact in the Greek of St Luke (1:28, 30), but subsequently abandoned, altogether regrettably, for it is only therein that the secret meaning is revealed. In Hebrew, Mariam is written MRIM, with the customary Hebrew omission of the vowels (I or Y, called *yod,* is a semi-consonant), which do not count in the interpretation, as it depends solely upon the consonants. The interpretation itself is based on the fact, re-discovered in the eighteenth century by Fabre d'Olivet and made known in his book *The Hebrew Tongue Restored,* that the written letters of Hebrew were originally hieroglyphs signifying principial or cosmic realities. His work was continued, refined, and completed by E.A. Chauvet in his monumental 4 volume *Ésotérisme de la Genèse,* published between 1946 and 1948, a work that has unfortunately remained little known and very seldom used. Thus the meaning of the name MRIM is revealed through an analysis of the meanings of each of its four letters and their internal relationships. The word divides into two parts: MIM and R. By articulating the vowel *a* in the first component, we obtain *Maim,* which means 'the waters' or 'water'; the M (*mem*), the form of which in Hebrew is that of a maternal breast, is the hierogram of passivity, of pure receptivity, one of the most widely distributed symbols of which is precisely water, whence the Hebrew plural *Maim* with the reinforcement created through the doubling of the M. Let us note in passing that in ancient Egyptian, 'water' was called *mou,* a term apparently of the same root, and whose hieroglyph is ⋀⋀⋀⋀⋀, a schematic representation of waves on the surface of water, the abridged form of which is none other than our M, with vertical sides, which in the past, however, often appeared as ⋀⋀, particularly in Greek inscriptions.

Returning to the word MRIM, let us note that I or Y (*yod*) is the hierogram of paternal energy, activity in itself and, at the principial level, Divine Activity. The letter *yod* is, moreover, found in the divine Names YHWH and YH. The R (*resh*) hierogram, in its Hebrew form, shows an erect serpent about to strike, and is the sign of energy/force which gathers momentum in order to deploy itself, so that the group RI translates the universal irradiation of divine energy. And profound meaning even extends to the difference between the two M's in the word, for if the first represents the maternal breast and pure passivity, the second, at the end of the word, represents receptive maternal power now become reproductive under the paternal impetus, and completing the emissive power. The name MaRIaM thus translates nothing less than the creative act: RI is the emission *ad extra* of Divine Energy, deploying itself in Substance, M, that is to say the totality of potentialities and the receptive milieu, the *Materia prima*, symbolized by the maternal breast of the hierogram and, on the cosmic plane, by the Primordial Waters, as shown in the first verses of Genesis (1:2), 'The Spirit of God moved upon the waters.' The Name of Mary is thus, after its fashion, a Divine Name, relating to divine creative activity, which means that Mary is a manifestation of this Divine Name. In short, it perfectly translates the divine Bi-unity, *Purusha-Prakriti*, God-*Materia prima*, God-*Shakti*, God-Principial Nature; in briefest form, it is an onomastic resume of creation *in divinis*. In passing, we can see how it was possible to express a whole metaphysical or cosmological doctrine synthetically in a single short formula by using the resources of a sacred language, such as Hebrew.

If we have gone into this matter at some length, it is because of the importance of the Name of Mary in both theology and liturgy. This is explained by the fact that in the Judeo-Christian tradition, as in all the great traditions (but perhaps more so in the Semitic traditions), a name is considered to be an expression of the very person or thing, so that we immediately see the importance it assumes when it is a matter of a Divine Name, expressing a divine Aspect or Quality, or mode of manifestation of the Divinity. Thus the Roman liturgy celebrates a Feast of the Holy Name of Jesus within the octave of Christmas, and, as already noted, a parallel Feast of the

Holy Name of Mary on 12 September, four days after her nativity. Let us further note that only the Names of Jesus and Mary are celebrated by liturgical feasts, which is added proof, if it were needed, of the divine character of the Name of Mary.

Let us return to the profound meaning revealed by the hierogrammatic analysis of this Name. The astonishing relationship that it immediately evokes between the nature of the Virgin and her role in the mystery of the Incarnation will no doubt have been noted. As 'Universal Mother', she is the 'Primordial Water' upon which the Spirit of God moved, and, at the moment of the Annunciation, the angel tells her: 'The Holy Spirit shall come upon thee and the power of the Most High shall overshadow thee' (Luke 1:35). The words of the angel are almost exactly those of the passage in Genesis that says, 'The Spirit of God *overshadowed* the waters.' We modify the usual translation in this way, following Chauvet, for the term employed by the Angel (*episkiasei* in Greek) means 'to overshadow', with the connotation of 'to incubate', or 'fecundate', exactly like the verb *merakhepheth* in the *Genesis* text of Moses, which is incorrectly translated as 'moved', while the complete verse is: *rouah Elohim merakhepheth al phenel ha-maim.* Thus the Messiah's conception in Mary's womb is effected in a manner totally analogous to the creation of the world. We shall see the reason for this later.

This parallel between the Name of Mary and the fecundation of the Primordial Waters at the origin of the cosmogonic process described by *Genesis* takes us back to what was said in the previous chapter on the symbolism of water, which, together with the symbolism of the earth, provides the Marian liturgy with so many of its images. These two symbols will now find their ultimate and profound justification in light of what has just been set forth.

The waters symbolize the totality of virtualities; they are like the womb of the possibilities of existence. Principle of the undifferentiated and virtual, water is the basis of all cosmic manifestation and the receptacle of seeds. By that very fact it is thus the entirely appropriate symbol of Primordial Substance, of the Feminine Principle, *Prakriti*, the *Magna Mater* in all her forms, who, under her Indian name of *Maha Devi*, declares in the *Devi Upanishad*:

I was born in water, in the depths of the ocean; he who knows this, reaches the abode of Devi. ... It was I who, at the beginning, created the father of this world.

The physical quality underlying this symbolism is the plasticity of water, which, like *Materia prima,* is absolutely shapeless, but also, like it, capable of assuming every shape; it is 'virgin' and thus, in itself, perfectly 'pure' and 'immaculate', *Virgo immaculata integra et casta.* And to this physical quality corresponds a quality of behavior, that of submission, perfect submission to activity exercised upon it, which is a beautiful image of the submission of the Virgin Mary to the Divine Will, she who wished only to 'serve': *Ecce ancilla Domini, fiat mihi secundum verbum tuum* [Behold the handmaid of the Lord, be it done to me according to thy word]; such was her response to the messenger of God, and in her *Magnificat* she glories, so to speak, in her humility: 'My soul doth magnify the Lord . . . for He hath regarded the lowliness of his handmaiden.'

The purity and humility of 'our sister water', as St Francis called it, makes of it the reflective element par excellence, a natural mirror. What a marvelous sight it is to see the heavens reflected in the waters of a tranquil lake! And poets, who know instinctively to pass from the visible to the invisible, have felt that there is something of the sacred in this sight, and so we have Victor Hugo saying, in these verses from *The Sorrow of Olympius*:

> Long he gazed on the fine forms
> Taken by nature in quiet fields:
> Dreaming till even;
> All day long in the ravine roaming,
> By turns the face of heaven admiring
> And the lake, mirror divine!

How is it possible not to see in these last two lines the image of God the Creator reflecting Himself in primordial Nature? And so we understand better the invocation *Speculum Justitiae* addressed to Mary: 'Mirror of Justice', Justice here signifying, according to its Scriptural meaning, 'Holiness', the Holiness of God. 'Virgin' water, perfectly 'pure' and perfectly 'submissive', Mary is, like a tranquil lake, a 'divine mirror', the mirror of the Creator.

But there is not only the calm water of tranquil lakes; there is also the gushing and bounding water of springs and fountains, their movement being the expression of the powerful energies they contain; for water, as one of the cosmic forms of *Materia prima*, receives creative energy in its motionless submission, and having thereby become 'Shakti', is in turn made creator. Water is 'living water', the 'water of life', which fecundates the earth through all the energies it has received, and which it distributes in turn—whence all the springs, fountains, and wells associated with the presence of the Virgin. She is the 'Sealed Fountain' spoken of in the *Song of Songs* (4:2) which, ultimately, is none other than the original source mentioned in Genesis (2:6): 'But there went up a mist from the earth, and watered the whole face of the ground.' Grillot de Givry was certainly correct, in his beautiful book *Lourdes ville initiatique*, when he said that the verse relates to the state of purity of creation when it was still in direct communion with the 'Source of Life', a state which was lost after the 'Fall', but regained after the Redemption; and he adds that 'Mary sustains that Source, as she does the springs and fountains of her sanctuaries,' which have purifying and healing properties, as we have already seen.

We find analogous characteristics and qualities in the earth, that other symbol associated with the Great Mother. It is sometimes considered a less noble element than water, and, *a fortiori*, than air and fire. No doubt this 'negative' symbolism results from being situated 'down below', at the point furthest away from 'Heaven', which, being 'on high', is where the divine world is situated, and because of this, the image of earth may suggest descent, heaviness and shadows, even the domain of death. However it also has a 'positive' symbolism, being the image of stability, fertility, substantiality, and, consequently, purity, which is manifested by the just mentioned springs of water; and substantiality further implies profundity and power. Besides, the 'inferior' position of earth at the so to speak lowest level of the cosmos, is, by contrast, rich in the fundamental quality of *humility*, which in fact takes its name from the word *humus* meaning 'earth', and is the pre-eminent characteristic of *Materia prima* and its human manifestation, the Most-Holy Mother of God. We have here an example of 'inverse symbolism', in which

an object of the most elementary cosmic order is qualified to represent a reality of the highest ontological or spiritual order.

The power of suggestion of the element 'earth' is such that more
often than not it has been chosen to represent sensible 'matter', both
in its 'plastic' form, as for instance potter's clay, which, like water, is
ready to assume different shapes, and in its hard and resistant form,
as stone, or marble, which, while being the most eloquent image of
substantiality and stability, and, spiritually speaking, safety—the
solid base of salvation—is, in spite of all, still disposed to lend itself
to a form, in the hands of a sculptor, for example. But earth above
all, the wide earth, the essential constituent of our world here
below, is 'Mother', the womb that receives seeds in order to develop
them. Water precedes creation and produces seeds, earth receives
them in its womb and produces and develops living forms.

Once again, how is it possible not to recognize the virtues of
Mary in this? The living forms of this world take root in the womb
of the earth, and this, we might say, borrowing an expression of Fr
Sergei Bulgakov, is a 'cryptogram of the Dei-Maternity wherein the
God-Man, the supreme goal of the whole created world, is born.'
Like *Prakriti*, the Holy Virgin is the earth; she is 'Mother, the moist
earth', to quote Dostoyevsky. And nowhere is this assimilation more
apparent than in the icon of the Nativity where she is presented in
two forms; as herself, reclining on the very earth itself, a truly Dem-
etrian figure, and as the grotto, the well-known chthonic image,
which we find at Lourdes, representing the womb of Mother Earth
and sheltering Jesus; she is thus presented simultaneously under her
human aspect and in her cosmic dimension.

We need to be very clear about what is meant when we way that
Mary 'is' the earth, for some would have it that in so doing we
reduce the Virgin to nothing but an image of a cosmic reality, a not
unfounded fear, for, unfortunately, this is how she is understood by
many people who pride themselves on their intellectuality. And
here we have the occasion to explain once and for all the meaning of
symbolism and how it works. When it is said that 'Mary is the earth',
this should be understood as 'theological metonymy', as we have
termed it in another work, and which Plutarch analyzed perfectly in
his treatise *On Isis and Osiris*. Criticizing, precisely, the materialistic

exegeses which say that 'Demeter is the ear of wheat' in the sense of she 'is only the ear of wheat', he remarked that this is to thereby falsifies religious truth and end in idolatry. According to him, we say that 'Demeter is the ear', in the same way that we say 'to play Menander' meaning 'to play the comedies of Menander', or, again, 'that is in Menander'.

Metonymy arises from properly-understood symbolism, in the traditional sense of the word: a symbol has ontological value, certainly, when understood in the 'vertical' direction, that is to say the one that links all the aspects of being together and causes a higher reality to be reflected in a lower one. In this way there is an analogy of being between the two and it can be said that the inferior reality 'is' the superior reality, which means precisely that it manifests it and enables a re-ascent to it. But it is obvious that the two are not absolutely identical, for in that case they would be but one.

Having completed this long, but necessary digression, let us return to the symbolism of earth itself as it applies to the Virgin. Now, grafted onto the inverse symbolism of the earth just analyzed above, is the color black, the color of the images of the Virgin that constitute the very starting point for this study.

As is the case with many symbols, the color black presents two opposing aspects, one benefic and the other malefic. The more usually envisaged malefic aspect recalls, at the material level, night, with its shadows and their attendant dangers, as opposed to the light of day; at the psychological level, ignorance, blindness, heaviness, and materiality; and at the level of the spirit, the denial of light and spiritual intelligence, even Satanism. Under its benefic aspect, on the other hand, black symbolizes mystery, the inexpressible and ineffable, and inwardness, particularly in connection with Knowledge.

Obviously, the black representations of the Virgin should be considered under this latter aspect, and immediately we recognize in the symbolism of the color black the principal characteristics and attributes of the Virgin already mentioned. First and foremost, we have the chthonic character of Mary as she is likened to the earth, for black evokes not only its surface, which more often than not is dark, but more especially its inwardness, its mysterious depth, which is revealed at the surface in grottoes and caverns, those privileged places of manifestation of the Virgin, and their ritual substitutes, crypts. These places recall the 'womb' of the earth, where life develops in 'darkness', and thus immediately refers us to the maternal womb; we could also say to the womb of the waters, whose depths are the image of the dark Primordial Waters. The maternal womb is related to the mystery of life, the gestation of wheat in the earth being the image of that of the embryo in the belly of the mother. The blackness of the earth, like that of deep waters, also has two senses: its visible color, or inwardness, and the mystery of the hidden gestation of life. And perhaps in connection with the color black we should recall here the relationship of the earth and deep waters to the moon, which we have already discussed, for there is a 'dark moon' during the periods of obscurity of the orb when it acts upon gestation, and, as we have seen, for this reason chthonic divine entities are also lunar entities, as is, for example, Artemis-Diana. Similarly, we can also mention the 'black sun', as the winter solstice was called in the past, which is analogous in its own sphere to the 'black stone', about which more in a moment. The 'black sun' is the sun of Christmas, the sun, so to speak, of Christmas night, the Virgin having traditionally given birth to Jesus at 'midnight', in the 'grotto' at Bethlehem, as the Offertory of the Mass for the octave of the feast has it.

> While all things were in quiet silence, and the night was in the midst of her course, Thy almighty Word, O Lord, came down from heaven from Thy royal throne (Wisd. 18:14–15).

Moreover, the traditional symbol of the 'midnight sun' is also related to the birth of Christ. At any rate, it is difficult not to see a connection between the 'black sun' and the Black Virgin, so often called *Virgo paritura*, the 'Virgin about to give birth'.

Under its black aspect, the earth symbolizes the substantial pole of manifestation at the very lowest rung of the ladder of being. This is what has been called its 'negative' symbolism, but, as has also been said, if we consider the summit of the ladder, the symbolism is inverted and becomes 'positive', because we then meet with the upper substantial pole of creation, namely *Materia prima*, that is *materia paritura*, for which the color black is also appropriate. This color is the image of the indistinction of Substance, which is non-manifested, just as, at the lower substantial pole, cosmic matter is also hidden from the senses in 'imitation' of the upper pole. Let us mention in passing that the 'Black Stone' of the Kaaba also has this meaning as did the Black Stone at Ephesus considered as an aniconic image of the Great Mother. Thus black symbolizes Wisdom from On-High, as the 'feminine' pole of manifestation, and for that very reason the *Black Virgin is in a way the manifestation of the non-manifested*. Let us quickly add that this is always the case with the Virgin Mary, irrespective of the color attributed to her, but that black evidently indicates this aspect of her nature in a particularly striking way.

Having arrived at this point in our reflections, we should now be in a position to clarify and justify the working hypothesis set forth at the start, by means of which we proposed to explain how Mary was able to succeed to the various earlier forms of the *Magna Mater*, and also to justify this practical quasi-assimilation. It was a question of seeing whether the term 'goddess' was appropriate for the Virgin, and if so, what its actual scope would be.

As already mentioned, this label is theologically unacceptable because, from the perspective of theology, the terms 'god' and 'goddess' are held to designate personalities of the same nature and, in a way, of the same level as the Supreme God, to whom they would be inadmissible 'rivals', which is, from this same perspective, what condemns polytheism. But we have likewise already indicated that such a position is unsustainable for the simple reason that it rests on a contradictory notion. In any case, Mary is not a 'divine person' like Christ, since what she incarnates is not a divine 'person' but an ontological principle, *Materia prima*. It is this that is the archetype of the human person of Mary, and it is this principle alone that belongs incontestably and entirely to the divine. Under its active form it is the *Shakti*, which is not a second divinity equal to the first, but rather its 'feminine' and 'substantial' aspect that enables it, in creating, to manifest itself. As already indicated, we believe the concept appropriate to define the status of Mary is that of 'feminine avatara', for an avatara can be the descent not only of a divine 'person', but also of a divine 'aspect' or 'name', which is precisely the case

87

with Mary. Within a polytheistic perspective, the Virgin would definitely be called a 'goddess' to the extent that the *Shakti* is a goddess and considered able to appear visibly in a human person.

This is perhaps the occasion to indicate the role of mythological language in polytheism. When speaking of ontological and metaphysical 'principles', it can be asked whether or not they are real beings. The answer is yes and no. Existing objectively as modes of being and action of the unique Reality, they are certainly real beings, and not 'things' or 'abstractions'; on the other hand, they are not 'persons'. In polytheism, however, they are 'personified', and this practice, which constitutes mythological language, has the altogether beneficial effect of forcing the mind not to see these principles as mere 'abstractions', as is the case with the usual philosophical approach, including Aristotelianism.

Accordingly, in the language of Hinduism, we could say that the Virgin is the *Shakti*, or the *Maya* of God, which in Christian language is Wisdom or Sophia, the biblical and liturgical reality applied to Mary and constituting our starting point, and which we are now able to see in its full meaning and all its profundity. Thus Wisdom, the exact Judaeo-Christian parallel to the *Shakti*, assumes, in passing via polytheism, an ontological consistency which, at first sight, was hardly apparent in the usual context where it is applied to the Virgin. And at the same time, our initial hypothesis, now verified, so it seems to us, has the double advantage of explaining on the historical plane the profound reason for the substitution of the Marian cult for that of the Great Mother and, on the properly spiritual plane, of giving a real insight into the depths of the Marian Mystery.

This Mystery, which in its inmost recesses is organically bound up with the avataric nature of Mary, is deployed outwardly on three planes: Creation, the Incarnation, and the spiritual life of the human individual.

Religious thought practically never addresses the study of the first and does not really take into consideration the cosmic aspect of the Mystery of the Virgin, at least today, for in the Middle Ages things were obviously quite different; if this were not so, we would have neither the Black Virgin, nor the multitude of Marian invocations we have encountered derived from the visible world to indicate the various attributes of Mary. This neglect on the part of ordinary Marian theology is altogether unfortunate, and all the more surprising at a time like ours when the responsible authorities are so eager to emphasize the 'incarnational' and 'carnal' nature of the Christian message.

We have just said that black representations of the Virgin aim in particular to recall the chthonic character of Mary, an aspect that should not be forgotten. It is important, in fact, not to 'relegate' her to Heaven, making of her a purely celestial being; it is important to keep her on earth, and all the more so today when she has so often expressed her desire to be manifested here. For if it is true that Christianity is indeed an 'incarnate' religion, this implies that its practice includes the integration of the faithful into the 'earth', in all senses of this term, starting with the most obvious, that of the 'soil', which has always been the great educator of man. Man needs to be reintegrated into cosmic reality, from which modern pseudo-civilization has almost entirely cut him off. This reintegration begins with a marriage to the earth in its sacred reality, and, as we shall see later on, Mary has an essential role to play in this. Today, man is in the process of exhausting rural civilization for economic gain; now, a country that can no longer count upon its peasantry is doomed. The peasant, in fact, is the one who, when the rest depart, maintains the earth; without him, a country risks sinking into barbarity. The Virgin Mary is she who maintains the motherland, which is why rural folk and shepherds have always accorded her great devotion.

That said, it is obvious that the Virgin embraces all of cosmic reality, all of Nature, as already mentioned: she is Nature made woman, the human manifestation of Principial Nature, of *Prakriti*, which is none other than the content of creative Divine Thought, the 'ideas', in the Platonic sense, or archetypes of different beings projected into *Materia prima*. In as much as she personifies Universal Substance, the Virgin is the perfect mirror of Creation in God and of His holiness, *Speculum Justitiae*, 'Mirror of Justice'; she is Nature in its original purity, the Divine Femininity upon which the Glory of the Spirit shines, Primordial Nature, Holy Wisdom. This Nature in God is exactly the same as it is in the world, realized exteriorly outside of

Him, except for the aspect of becoming, which, according to Plato's expression concerning 'time', makes of this visible world 'the moving image of eternity'; also except—obviously—for the possibility of 'falling', which is inherent in becoming. This is *Natura naturans, Materia prima* fecundated by the Divine Spirit, which produces *Natura naturata*, effectuated, visible, tangible Nature, the 'mirror' of Principial Nature. Mary is this Principial Nature, *Natura naturans, Prakriti*. And it seems that what we shall intentionally call the 'heavenly generation' of the Virgin is well expressed in these verses of the *Magnificat*, spoken by Mary before Elizabeth:

> My spirit hath rejoiced in God my Savior,
> For he hath regarded the lowliness of his handmaiden,
> For behold from henceforth, all generations shall call me blessed,
> For he that is mighty hath done to me great things. . . .

Quite obviously these words apply to Christ's conception, but they can also refer to the celestial origin of the Virgin. The 'lowliness of the handmaiden' applies perfectly to the nature of *Materia prima*, which is perfectly 'humble', because it is fundamentally 'that which is not', destitute of all being, but 'handmaiden', that is, totally offered and submissive to the effluvia of the Spirit; and, precisely on account of this 'poverty' and 'submission', the Spirit accomplishes 'great things' in her, that is to say the whole of Creation, because this total poverty, this 'emptiness' apt to receive all forms and to be inexhaustibly impregnated with them while remaining 'virgin' and 'immaculate'—these 'great things', refer us to beauty as to the multiplicity of universal Creation.

These reflections explain the initially astonishing title, 'Spouse of God', given to the Virgin in the litanies of the Acathist. This form of address takes us back to the metaphysical pair expressed in mythological language by the two 'personages' *Purusha* and *Prakriti*, the Active Principle of God and the Passive, Feminine Principle upon which creative activity is exercised, the Bi-Unity containing the macrocosmic mystery of the Creation, which can quite legitimately be expressed in the symbol of marriage.

Moreover, this making of Mary the Spouse of God reminds us of the well-known parallels previously encountered in the various hypostases of the *Magna Mater*, such as Ishtar in the Near East, or, in India, Kali, the 'Black', this being one of the names of the Maha Devi, the 'Great Goddess', who is also both 'virgin' and 'spouse'. As *Materia prima*, or pure submission to the Creative Will, the Virgin 'espouses' the Creator Spirit, offering him her total Passivity in order that he may manifest his Activity therein. As 'spouse', Mary 'gives birth' to the world, which is why she has on many occasions been called 'Co-Creatrix', a term marvelously expressive of her role within the pair *Purusha-Prakriti*. In a way she incarnates Principial Nature, and in so doing, integrally restores visible nature by communicating her beauty to it, as is declared in St John Damascene's hymn included in the great Byzantine Liturgy of St Basil: 'Oh Sanctified Temple, Spiritual Garden, Virginal Glory.... Oh full of grace, all Creation rejoices in thee.' Another hymn, belonging this time to the Latin liturgy, tells in similar accents of the kind of renewal that is brought about in the world by the appearance of Mary:

> All beautiful are you (*Tota pulchra es*), Oh Mary, all beautiful, and in you there is no stain.... Like a radiant dawn you advance, bringing in the joy of salvation. Oh shining Gate of Light, from you it is that Christ God, Sun of Justice, has come forth. Like a lily among thorns, oh blessed Virgin, such are you among the daughters of men. Your garments shine like the snow, your face like the sun. In you the hope of life and virtue lives, in you the whole grace of life and truth. We hasten to the sweet fragrance of your perfumes, which carry us away. Closed garden, sealed fountain, Mother of God and paradise of grace. The rain has withdrawn and gone away, winter has passed and flowers have already appeared. A voice is to be heard on earth, a very gentle voice: the voice of the turtle, the voice of the dove. Spread your wings, oh beautiful dove! Arise, make haste and come.

The Virgin is also called 'Queen of the World', *Regina mundi*, as she appeared in the already oft-cited passage from Revelations (11:19; 12:1), which furnishes the epistle for the mass of 11 February, the Feast of the Apparition of Mary at Lourdes:

And the temple of God was opened in heaven, and there was seen in his temple the ark of his testament. . . . And there appeared a great wonder in heaven, a woman clothed with the sun. . . .

Now it is interesting to note that this is the same figure as that of the third arcanum of the Tarot, called the *Empress*, who is depicted carrying a scepter, with her head surrounded by twelve stars and her feet on the crescent moon. This arcanum plays an important role in hermeticism, for it corresponds to 'Universal Mercury', another name for Universal Substance, which takes us back to the heart of the cosmic and supra-cosmic Mystery of the Virgin. Mary is truly Queen and Empress, for in her eternal being, as generative cosmic Substance, 'virgin' and 'mother', she presides over the whole universe, being the Rectrix of primordial energies and secondary causes.

This is also the meaning of another of her titles, 'Jacob's Ladder'. One is familiar with the passage from Genesis (28:12 ff.) recounting an episode in the life of the Patriarch:

And he dreamed, and behold a ladder set up on the earth, and the top of it reached to heaven: and behold the angels of God ascending and descending on it. And, behold, the Lord stood above it. . .

This ladder is evidently an image of the universe, from its base, the earth, even to its summit, God, and thereby an ontologically and metaphysically important symbol of the deployment of the multiple states of Being, from the lowest, represented by the earth, to the highest, that of pure Being, with the angels personifying the intermediary states above that of the terrestrial human. Thus, to call the Virgin 'Jacob's Ladder' amounts to saying that she has integrated in herself all ontological levels, up to the 'divine region'. This is another way of saying that she is 'Queen of the World', 'Queen of Heaven' and also 'Queen of the Angels'.

In all these titles, Mary is comparable to the Shekhina; this was alluded to earlier in the chapter by recalling that the Shekhina, the feminine personification of the Presence or Immanence of God in the universe, is very close to the notion of the Shakti, and is called 'the Queen', the feminine aspect of the Divinity uniting with 'the King'. In the Jewish tradition, the Shekhina, which is the synthesis of the sephiroth—the divine energies acting in the universe—is called the 'Governess' and 'Rectrix', a function which, as noted above, belongs to the Virgin as 'Queen of the World'; finally the Shekhina, like Mary, is the divine 'Glory' in which the Beauty and Purity of the Eternal and Divine Feminine is objectified. *Tota pulchra es.*

There is no rupture between the cosmic role of the Virgin and her role in the mystery of the Incarnation, for creation itself and the incarnation of the divine Word are effectively parallel and analogous to each other. Creation is, in fact, the *macrocosmic* incarnation of the Word, in whom are found the archetypes of all beings constituting Creation, while His descent in human form is the *microcosmic* incarnation; the first is operated through the projection of the archetypes into Universal Substance, *Materia prima*, symbolized by the 'Waters' of Genesis; the second takes place within the Virgin, who, as an earthly woman, is herself the manifestation, the *avatara*, of Universal Substance.

And herein lies the explanation of what is called the *mystery of the Immaculate Conception*: only a perfectly virgin creature could be the human mother of the Uncreated; only perfect 'Emptiness' could contain 'Fullness'. This is why Mary needed to 'be' *Materia prima.* Within manifestation, the individual being forgets the bond linking it to its archetype, thereby committing what theologians call 'original sin', while Mary, on the other hand, identified in her conception with Universal Substance, is 'exempted' from original sin, this being called a 'privilege' in the perspective and language of theology. Indeed, theology considers only the earthly woman when dealing with the Virgin, which is justifiable from a strictly monotheistic point of view, although in all honesty its explanation of the Immaculate Conception is not entirely satisfactory, for 'exemption' from sin would not in every respect constitute the absolute purity necessary to receive the direct contact in her womb of Him who, St Paul tells us, possesses the 'fullness of divinity'. A simple earthly woman, even if she were in the state of Eve before the Fall, would not be able to come into immediate contact with the Divinity without being destroyed, for if it is true that 'one cannot simply *see* God without dying' (Exod. 33:20), what is to be said about receiving Him integrally within oneself?

What God did when, in the anthropomorphic language of theology, He 'prepared' the person of Mary, was to identify her with the Eternal Feminine that is in Himself, with this Universal Substance in which He creates, and to make of her, as we have already said, the archetype of this unique woman. It is this that constitutes her Immaculate Conception, which obviously includes the exemption from sin, but also signifies far more. We have here new proof of her eternal generation and of the avataric character of her appearance as an earthly woman.

However, reflection on this initial observation will oblige us to go much further and scrutinize the meaning of the Immaculate Conception in all its fullness. For all that, the Holy Virgin herself invites us to do so: Pope Pius IX, in defining the ancient belief of the Church in dogmatic form in 1854, triggered—if we may be permitted to so speak—the declaration of the Virgin herself four years later, on 25 March, 1858, 'I am the Immaculate Conception', confirming his action before Bernadette and the world. What is more, it seems clear that neither at the time nor since has the vast majority of Christians, including their hierarchy, suspected the tremendous importance of these words of Mary. In his already cited book, *La charité profanée*, Jean Borella did not hesitate to say that they constitute 'the major theological event of modern times.' We are completely in agreement and even believe that this major importance is not restricted to modern times, but that the words are one of the major theological events in the history of Christianity, for, as Grillot de Givry says in his work *Lourdes*, Mary's declaration is the revelation of 'the most formidable mystery', 'the Keystone of the macrocosmic edifice'. We shall see why!

Jean Borella has pointed out something essential in connection with the very form the Virgin gave her words, calling attention to what, although obvious, no one else has seen, namely, that she did not use the following words or something similar: 'My conception was immaculate,' or, perhaps, 'I was conceived an immaculate woman,' which would adequately translate the tenor of the dogma and correspond exactly to the belief of the Church and the faithful. Rather, Mary pronounced these stupendous words, 'I am the Immaculate Conception.' Truly, it is absolutely astonishing that no one has noticed that according to human logic and the rational point of view, it is absolutely impossible for a simple individual to claim to 'be a conception'. Indeed, how can an abstract noun expressing an idea or a fact be ascribed, as an attribute with onto-logical value, to an individual? Strictly speaking, such would be an aberrant and unacceptable statement. We certainly do not object to formulations such as 'this man is a mystery', or 'is an enigma', or something similar, in which the abstract substantive employed as attribute has, in reality, only an adjectival value equivalent to 'mys-terious', or 'enigmatic'. Thus, viewed under the bright light of the grammarian's critical gaze, the Virgin's declaration appears to be situated on a plane entirely transcending that of human thought, forcing us, by virtue of its being completely outside the rational norm, to consider it as charged with a tremendous revelation.

In fact, the notion of immaculate conception is not univocal; it cannot be limited to a designation of Mary's 'privilege' at her birth; we have already seen that it refers, on the principial plane, to *Materia prima* or Universal Substance, of which Mary is the living mir-ror. But it is necessary to go further or, rather, higher, to the supreme degree, that of the Godhead, the Absolute. At this degree the Immaculate Conception is the 'pure', therefore absolutely 'immaculate' 'conception' of every—even essential—determination and limitation that the Absolute assumes of Itself, insofar as It knows Itself as the Principle of every possible thing; it is the Infinity of Possibilities, Universal Possibility, which, as Energy of the Abso-lute, is the *Mahashakti*. Now, at the beginning of the chapter we saw that corresponding to the *Mahashakti* at a lower degree, that of Being, we have the *Shakti* of the personal God, which is what *Materia prima* is called when, fecundated by the divine principle, it becomes *Prakriti*. This latter is the reflection of the *Mahashakti* of the Supreme Principle, which is situated at the level of Beyond-Being, and in the final analysis, only exists—if we may use a term inappropriate here—because of it, so that we are forced to situate the Immaculate Conception of the Virgin, who is herself assimilated thereto, at the supreme degree. J. Borella, along with Abbé H. Stéphane, also did not hesitate to say that there is metaphysical identity between Universal Possibility as *Mahashakti* or *Shakti* of the supreme Divinity, and the Virgin Mary as 'Spouse and Mother of God', titles which thus gain a far greater resonance than that indicated earlier. Indeed, it was Mary herself who took pains to say it when she appeared at Lourdes, and since she affirmed it, we are obliged to admit that her prototype is the Divine Essence Itself insofar as It conceives the ideas of beings, that is, as *Mahashakti*, and that she is identified with It.

Such is the astounding revelation that resounded in the grotto at Lourdes. In her highest signification, Mary is the human personification and revelation of the unrevealed Godhead in its aspect of Infinity, as she is in other respects the human personification of *Materia prima* and Universal Nature. And note well that this personification corresponds exactly to that of Wisdom, Holy Wisdom, in its highest signification, that of the *Mahashakti*, this Wisdom being nothing other than the Immaculate Conception, which is the ultimate explanation for the attribution of this title to Mary.

All of this throws light upon the mystery of her immaculate birth. In his book *Amphitheater of Eternal Wisdom*, Khunrath explains that since Mary's celestial origin is immaculate, her earthly conception needed to be so as well; she was conceived without sin in the womb of Anna because she had first been conceived, according to Khunrath's own words, in 'the womb of the Godhead'.

The fundamental identity of the Virgin with *Mahashakti* explains her role in the birth of Christ.

We saw at the beginning of the chapter that *Mahashakti*, under the action of the Divine Essence, triggers the process of universal manifestation, or *Maya*, the first effect of which is the bringing forth of the personal God, Who is pure Being and the first determination, or rather auto-determination, of the undifferentiated and unknowable Absolute. Then comes the whole series of creatures, starting from *Prakriti*, the *Shakti* of the personal God, which, as the reflection of the *Maya* of the Supreme Principle on the plane of manifestation, is also called *Maya*. In order to distinguish the *Maya* of the Supreme Principle, identical with Wisdom or Sophia, from cosmological or lower *Maya*, the former is called *Maha-Maya*, or 'Great Maya'. The term 'Maya' has the precise meaning of 'Divine Art', the word 'art' being used in its original sense of creative or fabricating activity at any level. In short, *Maya* and *Maha-Maya* are used for *Shakti* and *Mahashakti* when one considers the *effect*, or result, of the one and the other.

It is through its *Shakti*, or *Mahashakti*, that the Absolute is eternally revealed to Itself; the Eternal Feminine is the 'mould' in which the Supreme God, the Beyond-Being, produces His epiphany as personal God, and in which the mystery of divine manifestation dwells, His Glory and Wisdom. Without the manifestation of His Glory and Wisdom, the Godhead would remain unknown and unknowable.

The Virgin's role in the Incarnation of Christ can be understood in the light of the above considerations. The divine Word could not have taken on human form without Mary, and she can be called 'Mother of God' in the sense intended by ordinary theology, that is to say on the human plane, because, on the supreme plane, her role is played by the Eternal Feminine, the *Mahashakti*, the *Maha-Maya* or Universal Manifestation, the Immaculate Conception, which eternally 'gives birth to God', since, as Denis the Areopagite says, the 'Godhead engenders God'. The supreme *Shakti*, which is *Maya* and *Wisdom*, the supreme activity of the Absolute and of Universal Possibility, is reflected in the Pure Passivity of *Prakriti*, also called *Maya*, otherwise called Principial Omnipotence in the Potentiality of *Materia prima*. The *Shakti*, or *Maya*, or, to use Christian terms, Wisdom or Sophia, is the mother of the *Avatara*, both as *Mahashakti* in the case of his eternal generation, and *Prakriti* or lower *Maya* in his birth in the world. By proclaiming herself the 'Immaculate Conception', the Virgin Mary, who is herself identified with *Mahamaya* and, at a lower level, with *Maya* or *Prakriti*, can be said to be 'Mother of God' not only in the human generation of God as Jesus, but also in His eternal generation. We could even say that it is only because she is 'Mother of God' in His eternal birth that she can be so in His human birth, which is what Meister Eckhart said:

Our Lady, before becoming Mother of God in His humanity, was Mother of God in His divinity, and the birth she gave Him in His divinity is represented by the birth as man He took in her' (*Sermon 8*, Evans).

Thus is resolved the ambiguity that previously attached to the title 'Mother of God', when considered only from the point of view of the human birth of Jesus.

Here we touch upon the very heart of the Marian Mystery, which, as stated in the introduction, is the principal subject of this study. And, given everything that has just been said, we can gauge the progress of this revelation during the course of Christian history: between Ephesus, 22 June, 431 and Lourdes, 25 March, 1858, what a distance traveled! The Holy Council declared Mary 'Mother of God', or Theotokos, as mother of the Incarnate Word, Jesus, and fourteen centuries later, she herself revealed the highest meaning of this title by proclaiming herself the 'Immaculate Conception', that is to say, her rootedness, if we may be allowed this term, in the supreme Divinity.

And ultimately, this is what is symbolized by the icon of the *Black Virgin*. As already noted, the dark color is the image of the unmanifest, of what remains hidden, and on this level corresponds to *Prakriti*, the universal Substance with which Mary is also identified. And the color black applies *a fortiori* to the supreme degree, it being the most hidden. The black of *Materia prima*, which is *potential indistinction*, is the reflection on a lower plane of the *principial non-distinction* of the Infinite, of *Mahashakti*, the divine Eternal Feminine, of the blackness of that 'dazzling Darkness', to use an expression of Denis the Areopagite. The black image is the icon of the *Magna Mater*, the *Maha-Devi* of India, who, under this relationship is called *Kali*, 'The Black', and who is addressed in the following terms:

You are the image of All . . . the mother of All. . . . Before things began you existed in the form of an *obscurity* beyond words and thought, and from you, through the creative desire of the supreme Brahma, the entire universe was born. . . . You are Kali, the first form of all things. . . . Resuming your *dark* and shapeless form after the dissolution (maha-pralaya), you remain unique, ineffable, inconceivable (*Maha Nirvana Tantra*).

If we consider the black and the white icons of the Virgin, we can say that the first symbolizes Infinity and the second absolute Purity, the two in a certain way being combined in the 'Constellation of the Virgin', the light of which glitters against the dark heavens, and in the mantle covering the majority of statues of Mary, a blue mantle—traditionally, blue is an attenuated black—studded with golden stars. Thus the symbolism of the black color of Marian statuary embraces the entire space extending from earth to heaven, from the darkness of the womb of the earth even to the super-essential Darkness of the Supreme Divinity.

If, for some, an 'enigma' of the Black Virgins exists, its solution is to be found here, together with the revelation of the depths of the Marian Mystery itself. Harking back to the history of the black statues of the Virgin, we find confirmation of the thesis that the advent of the Black Virgins was the joint effort of the secular intuition of the people nourished by memories of ancient goddesses, and the superior theology of the most enlightened monks. This type of image, espoused and spread by the monks, was able to communicate to those who understood, or at least sensed, what ordinary theology and the liturgy only allows to be intimated when they celebrate the Virgin's 'assumption' into heaven and coronation as 'Queen of the Angels', that is to say her being carried above the whole of creation, as 'earthly woman' become 'Heavenly Woman', and reuniting with her eternal origin, which thus finds itself manifested.

This is to say that, in the eyes of these monks, the Marian Mystery was of capital importance to Christians. In fact the role played by the Mother of God in man's destiny cannot be exaggerated. This question shall be considered in the following chapters, but here we are at a convenient point to show the foundations upon which it is based, enabling us to complete what has so far been said concerning the place of Mary in Christ's Incarnation and Redemption.

The Church has proclaimed the Virgin 'Co-Redemptrix' with Christ, in view of the fact that she is also 'Co-Creatrix'. In fact, as pointed out above, Redemption is Re-creation or Re-generation, a new creation or new birth for man and, indissolubly, for the whole cosmos. The role of woman in this regeneration is primordial, she having been at the very origin of the 'Fall'. Indeed, the Fall applied in the first place to woman, to Eve, and consisted in her not being able to remain faithful, as the lower feminine principle at the cosmic level, to the higher Feminine Principle, which she reflected; more precisely, as Grillot de Givry has clearly shown, she was unable to maintain *life*—and let us not forget that her name, Heva, means 'Life'—at the level at which she had been entrusted to do so. For Eve, the Fall consisted in separating herself from the higher Feminine Principle, which, moreover, was *alone* able to restore to woman her lost dignity and repair the fall of the entire world caused by the Fall of Eve. Otherwise put, since the fall of the macrocosm was brought about by the feminine part of the human microcosm, it was necessary that this feminine part participate in the universal regeneration; or, rather, that the regeneration be made to proceed from Woman by making her the mother of the divine Logos in its earthly descent.

In order to understand aright the Fall of Eve and her restoration by Mary, it is necessary to consider the double movement of *Maya*, or Nature, the feminine power. The first movement, that of 'descent', called *pravrithi-marga* in India, and corresponding to the Plotinian 'procession' or *proodos,* is 'descending Maya', and involves dropping from the higher, essential, pole to the lower, substantial pole of manifestation, at the end of which normally follows a second movement called 'ascending Maya', and re-ascension to the Principle. These two terms correspond fairly well to the distinction made by Fr Bulgakov between Sophia and fallen Sophia. However, in the course of this process, it can happen that at the end of the descent the force of the *Shakti* is detached from the Principle and is scattered indefinitely; this eventuality being due to the fact that within Universal Possibility, or *Mahashakti,* or *Mahamaya,* there is necessarily a negation of Being that constitutes the source of 'evil' and the possibility of a 'fall'.

This is specifically wherein lies the Fall of Eve, the result of 'descending Maya' overshooting the normal lower limit of its manifestation and rupturing the link with the divine world. The Marian Mystery, on the contrary, depends as F. Schuon has shown upon 'ascending Maya', wherein the feminine principle is not only regenerated, but becomes regenerative. Fallen Eve caused the obscuring of that part of the feminine principle destined for earth; Eve was 'virgin' in her spirit and her physical being, which was the virginity of the very principle of life; her Fall was like the death of the Cosmic Virgin, for she had sinned in her very virginity, and, as a result, brought about the victory of matter over spirit. Mary is the 'New Eve' because in her earthly manifestation she is the feminine principle kept pure and virgin, perfectly united to her eternal prototype, becoming thereby the visible and efficacious sign of the reintegration of the degenerate feminine principle into the higher one.

From this we see that the regeneration of Adam was not possible except through the regeneration of Eve, who had been the cause of his own fall. Besides, metaphysically, the New Eve is indissolubly linked to the New Adam. The Mystery of Redemption or Reintegration is the Mystery of *Theanthropy*, of God-Manhood, that is to say of the state of Man-God that man needs to attain following the Word Incarnate. Now, theanthropy is realized not by Jesus alone, but by Jesus *and* Mary, a point emphasized by Fr Bulgakov in his book *The Lamb of God*. The redemption, he says, can only be accomplished by Man *and* Woman so as to recover and re-establish the state before the Fall. And this, he adds, is why Mary is Co-Redemptrix, not only because she shared the sufferings of Christ, as is usually said, but first and foremost through her Immaculate Conception.

This is the truth referred to by the initially astonishing title 'Spouse of Christ', which title is found in the litany of the Acathist and has inspired certain plastic representations. Thus at Santa Maria Trastevere in Rome, the Virgin is clearly shown as Spouse of Christ, being seated with Him on one and the same throne, while He holds this indicative text from the Song of Songs (2:6): 'His left hand is under my head, and his right hand doth embrace me.' The title 'Spouse of Christ' is the synthetic expression of the statement that Mary is not only 'Mother' of Jesus but, together with him, also forms the *renewed and virginal pair of the New Adam and New Eve*. Although current piety is unaware of it, this spousal union is made explicit in the union of the 'Hearts of Jesus and Mary', which are not only those of Son and Mother, but also Husband and Wife.

This conception is related to the already mentioned Jewish doctrine of the Shekhina in which the latter, likened to the 'Queen', is united with the 'King' so as to ensure cosmic order, a union further expressed in the marriage of *Tiphereth*, the King, to *Malkuth*, another aspect of the Shekhina, which is then called the *Matrona* and, as such, is entitled 'Mediatrix'—an official title of the Virgin— and 'Receptacle of the blessings from On-High', which immediately calls to mind the Angel greeting Mary as 'full of grace'.

If this is now considered from the metaphysical standpoint, it will be noticed that the theanthropic couple is the reflection of the divine Dyad or Bi-Unity, *Purusha-Prakriti*, in the cosmic sphere, the sphere of Redemption. It will then be seen that, from this perspective, the theanthropic couple of the New Adam and New Eve is the reconstitution of the *Primordial Androgyne* so clearly described in the text from Genesis (1:27), which should always be kept in mind. In its manifestation in the visible order, the primordial androgyne, which belongs to the principial order, expresses itself in the virginal pair of the Man and Woman.

Before proceeding to look at the implications of this spousal union, let us note in passing that it explains a seemingly strange fact, namely that the names of the Virgin have equivalents in those of Christ: thus 'Queen of Heaven', 'King of Heaven', 'Queen of the world', 'King of the world', 'Wisdom', 'Morning Star' (2 Pet. 1:19 and Rev. 22:16 for Christ, who says 'I am the bright and morning star'). The same goes for the title 'Mother of Mercy', for Christ is called 'Rich in Mercy'. Once again, this parallelism is related to the Shekhina, which refers as much to Christ as to Mary. The connections between Christ and the Shekhina have been clearly brought to light in an important observation by Fr Bouyer, who, in his book *The Seat of Wisdom*, notes that in 'The Word was made flesh and dwelt among us' of St John's Gospel, the Greek verb used to designate the sojourn on earth of the Incarnate God, *eskenose*, which literally means 'has pitched his tent', is based on the tri-lettered root *skn*, which is exactly the Hebrew root *shkn* (for the sounds *s* and *sh* are transcribed by the same character) of the word Shekhina, designating the divine presence among men. It can hardly be imagined that the Apostle in writing his Gospel did not deliberately choose the verb in question, which constituted a veritable cryptogram, enabling whoever was able to recognize the Hebrew under the

Greek to understand that the Word Incarnate was the human manifestation of the Shekhina.

Thus, to return to the parallel names of Christ and the Virgin, it
is as if the Shekhina divided itself on the visible plane into the two
'actors' of the Redemption. Perhaps the most striking example of
this is that alongside the 'Mediator', who is Christ, Mary, as already
noted, is called 'Mediatrix', a title recognized officially by a special
feast on 31 May that honors her under this designation. 'It is God's
will that we have everything through Mary,' said St Bernard; grace
proceeds from the Holy Spirit, but it is through Mary that it reaches
mankind. St Bernard also says that Mary 'is the channel or aqueduct
whereby all the heavenly waters reach us.' Now it is instructive to
remember that this is precisely one of the principal functions of the
Shekhina under its name 'Matrona'. According to the Zohar,

All the messages sent here below by the supreme King pass
through the intermediary of the Matrona, and all the messages
sent to the supreme King from the world below first arrive at the
Matrona who transmits them to the supreme King. As a result,
the Matrona serves as intermediary to the world On-High in its
communication with the world below, and vice versa. Thus she
is the perfect *mediatrix* between Heaven and earth (*Zohar* III,
50B).

Other correspondences come to mind. For example, we know
that in creation the activity of the Shekhinah operates according to
the two pillars of the sephirotic tree, Rigor or Justice, and Mercy;
now Christ is simultaneously the Judge, the Lover of Justice, and
the Merciful, but, correspondingly, so also is the Virgin. For if she is
the 'Mother of Mercy', she also presents a formidable aspect that,
moreover, often appears in her black statues. Here, again, we should
consider the metaphysical point of view. The *Shakti*, the feminine
and maternal aspect of the Divine, is gentleness, tenderness, kindness, and joy, which succors, attracts, and offers blessings, but from
another angle she can appear terrible. In fact, beyond beauty, riches,
plenitude, etc., Universal Possibility implies the negation of Being
and the possibility of evil, whence the divine reaction which is manifested by Rigor and what the Scriptures call 'Divine Anger': this is

the terrible Shakti. In India, these two aspects belong to Kali, the 'Black', who is sometimes Bhavani and Ellamma, 'the Benevolent', and sometimes Kalama, 'the Terrible', and Durga, 'the Inaccessible'. Certainly, the contrast is not nearly so great with the Virgin Mary; although it nevertheless exists, it is too often forgotten. If she is full of love and mercy for 'men of good will', if she is the 'refuge of sinners', helping them repent, she is also terrible for all the enemies of God, both men and demons. Let us recall the epicleses cited in the last chapter: 'Powerful Virgin', 'terrible like an army ranged for battle', 'terror of enemies', 'lightning that destroys enemies', etc.

But the first title under which piety honors Mary is that of 'Mother', and let us not forget that if the Church has proclaimed her 'Mother of God', Theotokos, she also calls her 'Mother of men'. Under this last name she is also the New Eve, assuming, in order to exalt it, the destiny of the first Eve who was the 'Mother of the living' (Gen. 3:20), the unhappy mother, alas!, of the unhappy living. For individual man, redemption is the 'second birth' conferred upon him by baptismal initiation. Now, as we have often said, this second birth is ritually operated only through a 'return to the mother', that is to say to the origin, which is why the baptismal vessel has always been likened to a maternal womb. Baptismal initiation however, like all initiation, is virtual; it deposits a divine seed, issue of the Holy Spirit, which needs to enter a maternal womb in order to be born. It is Mary who welcomes those baptized into her womb and prepares them to actualize the virtue of baptismal initiation. In his book *Treatise on True Devotion to the Blessed Virgin*, St Grignon de Montfort wrote,

> St Augustine calls the Holy Virgin *forma Dei*, 'the mould of God', the mould adapted to form gods; he who is poured into this divine mould is soon formed and shaped in Jesus Christ and Jesus Christ in him; ... he will become God, since he is poured into the same mould that formed a God.

Baptism, together with the Eucharist, is indeed capable of endowing man with the Christic nature, of leading him to *theosis*, but only after he has been born of Mary, as Jesus wished when he said to St John and, through him, to all men: 'Son, behold thy mother.' This is also the meaning of the adage, officially recognized by the Church, *Ad Jesum per Mariam*, to Jesus through Mary. Following the Virgin in her 'assumption', man, then, can ascend to the very summit of the heavens, for if Mary is called 'Queen of the Angels' and 'Queen of the heavens', this means that, as earthly woman, she has traversed and recapitulated all the superior states of Being symbolized by the words 'heavens' and 'angels'—and in her 'Coronation' has rejoined the Divinity whence she issued, just as Jesus, after his resurrection, also, *as the first*, ascended as man 'above all the heavens' (Acts 1:10; Heb. 4:14) where he resides as the Divine Word to all eternity. This is also the meaning of 'Jacob's Ladder' and why, in the Acathist litany, the Virgin Mary is invoked as 'The ladder by which men ascend from earth to heaven.' The Virgin, as earthly woman, has integrated all the higher states of Being and has thereby become, along with Christ, the prototype of glorified humanity. So much so that, after death, there will be no need for him who, following Jesus' wish, has become 'son of Mary', to effectively traverse in the manner of a transmigration the multiplicity of superior states in order to attain deification, since, as 'son of Mary', and therefore 'son of God', he has already integrated them virtually.

This intimate cooperation of Mary in the integral fulfillment of the Christian spiritual life, which is none other than the 'Christification' of the faithful—the true Christian being, according to the traditional formula, 'another Christ' (*alter Christus*)—invites us to consider, in a different way from usual, the icon encountered at the beginning of our research, that of the 'Virgin in majesty', enthroned, presenting her son seated on her knees, as though issuing from her womb (*fructus ventri tui*); in the East, the corresponding icon, called the 'Virgin of the Sign', shows Mary with the Child *in* her open womb. The child, who is most certainly the Child-God, Jesus, is *also* the divine child that the elect should become 'in imitation of Christ', by passing through the womb of the Virgin. And in this regard, the *black statue* is particularly expressive, as we shall shortly see.

4

'I Am Black
But Beautiful'

Song of Songs 1:5

THE SPIRITUAL ROLE of Mary just mentioned leads us directly
to consider an important and characteristic aspect of the cult of the
Black Virgin, that of its connection to alchemy and the links
between the latter and the art of church-building. In *Le mystère des
cathedrals*, Fulcanelli writes that 'the Black Virgins, always installed
in a crypt, represented the matter upon which the alchemists were
to work,' an idea that at first sight may appear surprising and which
clearly calls for clarification; we shall return to it later. For the
moment, however, let us note that this connection between the
Black Virgin and alchemy was prefigured in Greco-Egyptian Hermeticism from its beginnings. The color black attributed to Isis was
expressly presented as the symbol of the 'Secret Doctrine.' In fact, in
the treatise entitled *Core Cosmu* (no. 23 of the *Corpus Hermeticum*)
—a title usually translated as 'The Cosmic Virgin', but nothing could
be less certain—Isis herself declares,

> Listen carefully, Horus my son, for here I tell you the secret doc-
> trine [*Crypte theoria*] that my grandfather Kamephis learnt from
> Hermes . . . and I from Kamephis, when he honored me with the
> gift of perfect Blackness [*teleio melani*].

Kamephis is the Grecianized form of the Egyptian *ka-mut-ef*, a
divine epithet attributed to several divinities during the Pharonic
era, and which in the Late Period came to indicate a completely separate god. As Kamephis is called 'The Ancestor before Everything' in

the sequel to the treatise in question, it is probable that in this context the name indicated the primordial god Amun, sometimes called *Amun kamutef*. This detail is interesting for it shows the divine origin of the Hermetic 'Secret Doctrine', including alchemy, which forms an important part of it. Moreover, another alchemical text (*Corpus des alchemistes grecs*, pp 28–35), also presenting itself as a revelation of Isis to Horus, tells us that Isis went to the temple of Horus at Edfu to receive the secrets of alchemy there. This information concerning the origin of the Secret Doctrine should be kept in mind, for what it expresses in mythological language amounts to saying that this science, as with all traditional sciences, is founded upon principles based in metaphysics.

All of this permits us to brush aside the prejudices regarding alchemy, particularly in Catholic circles where, even today, it is included among more or less 'accursed' sciences, despite its having been studied or practiced by no less reputable figures than St Albert the Great, St Thomas Aquinas, and the famous Gerbert who became Pope Sylvester II.

In the past, alchemy, together with astrology, to which it is related, was one of the most frequently practiced traditional sciences. Its field is cosmology, and more especially mineral matter, or metals, but its essential, final aim is of a spiritual order. The goal of the 'Great Work' is to effect a way of redeeming matter and the material world; its method consists in purifying metallic substances, combining them, and raising their qualities to a higher pitch so as to hasten their development towards the perfect metallic state, that of gold. This development, in fact, is equally the goal of nature; natural transformation, however, is slow, and the work of the alchemist consists in collaborating with nature and aiding it by means of an activity that, in a very general way, God assigned to man from the beginning. Such is the final goal of alchemy. Its immediate goal is the acquisition of the 'Philosophers' Stone', which makes the transmutation of metals and their 'redemption' possible, this being the first step in a 'cosmic redemption', including, we shall see, a spiritual realization for man.

The basic principle of alchemical science is the unity of matter—a particular aspect of the unity of the world as a whole—and, as a direct consequence, the interpenetration of the material and spiritual orders through the medium of the subtle order. The alchemist works less upon material substances themselves than upon their latent energies; he aims to develop the 'seminal powers' sprung from the 'Universal Fluid', the *spiritus mundi*, which animate everything; the Philosophers' Stone in its turn constitutes the synthesis and visible aspect of these powers.

As with all operative traditional sciences, the alchemical method is based upon a repetition, or if one prefers, an imitation, of the cosmogonic act: the practitioner imitates and reproduces, at his own level, the process of creation *in illo tempore*. Now, this process is the result of the separation, followed by the union, of two fundamental principles expressing all oppositions and 'sympathies'—the Luminous-Fire or Spirit, and undifferentiated *Materia prima*—the creative *Fiat lux* (cf. in *Genesis* the Spirit moving on the waters and producing the creative light) being the vibration that sets in motion the cosmogonic process. In alchemy, these two principles are called *Sulphur*, the element related to fire, and *Mercury*, that related to water. These two elements denote not so much the material substances themselves that bear these names, as the material 'qualities' that at this level express the two higher principles found at the cosmogonic level.

Sulphur and Mercury, considered both as principles and in their materiality, are respectively called 'male' and 'female'. We recognize here an aspect of the Divine Bi-unity, the manifestations of which have occupied us throughout our research.

The 'Great Work' of alchemy consists in realizing as perfectly as possible the harmonious union of Sulphur and Mercury, the Masculine and Feminine, called the 'hermetic marriage', which allows access to the Philosophers' Stone.

Initially the operation consists in procuring the matter for the Philosophers' Stone, in forming a new body by uniting the two principles that have first been extracted in a pure state, for the Stone has to be born of Sulphur and Mercury. The 'remote matter', also called 'primal earth' by alchemists, which is the 'subject of the Work', is described in certain texts as 'an ore-like material buried beneath a rocky mass' or as 'a *black* stone-like substance'. This shapeless matter is nevertheless precious, because it contains all the possibilities of transmutation. Its processing involves delicate operations that have to take into account the relationships of metals to the four elements, the four qualities of Nature, the fixed and the volatile etc., matters which need not occupy us now, it being sufficient to recall the broad outlines of alchemical science. In practice, most alchemists obtained the raw material by reducing common gold and silver, these two substances being the richest in Sulphur (gold) and Mercury (silver); sometimes common mercury was added, it being rich in salt, the substance that facilitated the union of the first two.

Before starting, the two metals first had to be purified so that 'philosophers' gold and silver' could be obtained. By a dissolution, the two principles, Sulphur and Mercury, were extracted in the form of salts, which were then calcined and the residue dissolved in acids, and in this way a liquid was obtained, the 'proximate material' of the Work. This was enclosed in the 'Philosophers' Egg', a completely sealed ball of glass, which was heated on the athanor. Here, evaporations, condensations and crystallizations occurred during which the matter took on different colors, of which the principal, *Black, White,* and *Red,* served to denote the three main phases of the work.

In the first, called the 'black work' (*nigredo*), the matter was dissolved so as to release the two principles, Sulphur and Mercury, and there was a reduction to *Materia prima* in the shape of a sort of *black* 'stone' called the 'raven'. In the second phase, called the 'white work' (*albedo*), the 'hermetic' or 'philosophical marriage' of the two principles, called the 'King' and the 'Queen' took place. At this stage, the matter was called the 'Rebis' or the 'alchemical hermaphrodite', and the 'stone' gradually became *white.* Initially dead and black, it was reborn and named the 'swan', this resurrection being signaled by a luminous twinkling. In the third phase, the 'red work' (*rubedo*), the stone passed through all the colors of the rainbow and became a bright *red*; this was the *red stone,* the *Philosophers' Stone,* sometimes called the 'Phoenix', sometimes the 'Pelican', and sometimes the 'Young Crowned King' clothed in royal purple.

The Philosophers' Stone was the active condensation of the *spiritus mundi,* 'the origin of all things', also called *Azoth* (a cryptogram composed of the first and last letters of the Hebrew, Greek, and Latin alphabets: A common to all three, Z, the final letter of the Latin, O, the final of the Greek, and Th, the final of the Hebrew). The red mass mixed with melted gold was capable of transmuting metals. It also provided the 'Elixir of Longevity' or 'liquid Gold' used medicinally in spagyric medicine, but which, above all, symbolically denoted the famous *pharmakon athanasias,* or 'medicine of immortality', which, according to the 'Hermetic Writings', the Greco-Egyptian Isis gave to her son Horus, and in fact was none other than initiation into the 'mysteries' founded by her.

As already indicated, the Great Work carried out in the 'laboratory' was conceived as the tangible, physical support of an interior, spiritual activity capable of leading the practitioner to Knowledge and illumination. By correcting, or 'rectifying' oneself, one is to 'sublimate' the '*black* matter', that is to say the individuality of the fallen human state. In his *Archidoxus,* Paracelsus writes that 'a man who, by renouncing all sensuality and blindly obeying the will of God, has come to participate in the activity of the celestial intelligences' (for the right ordering of nature), 'thereby possesses the Philosophers' Stone.' Moreover, in R. Alleau's *Aspects de l'alchimie traditionnelle,* we read:

The masters of alchemy look upon the mineral Adam as the reflection of man and the universe in the mirror of nature. Through knowing the conditions of transformation of the metallic microcosm, man is able to discover and analogically understand the laws of his own metamorphosis. Through purifying and perfecting the 'Sage's Subject' (the matter of the Work), and by capturing and finally absorbing the energy from other worlds condensed by this mysterious Lodestone, the human being possesses a means to make the Light descend into the depths of his body and consciousness.

There is no reason, let it be said, to question the physical reality and efficacy of the procedures carried out in the laboratory. Rather, let us note again that they serve above all as a support for a parallel and analogous activity in the very person of the practitioner with a view to realizing a transformation of a spiritual order. In the 'black work' undertaken in the laboratory, the substances are 'dissolved' and reduced to the state of *Materia prima*. At the same time, the practitioner suffers the 'dissolution' of his individuality, which is purified and undergoes the ordeal of 'death': in the full sense, this is a 'mortification', a descent into the obscure layers of the self which are related to their macrocosmic analogies. This is the dissolution that leads the principles of the human being back to the impersonal macrocosmic roots from which they derive and by which they are fed. A light expands over the ambiguous lower world and transforms these shadowy figures into the precise forms of the higher world. Through distillation, 'mercury', vital energy, returns to the free state of an undetermined vital possibility; this is the conversion to *Materia prima* upon which the inner 'sulphur' can efficaciously work.

In the 'white work', 'sulphur' and 'mercury', that is, the masculine and feminine principles, the *animus* and *anima* of the human personality, are united harmoniously and give birth to the hermetic androgyne, the 'Hermetic Child', 'Son of the King', whose appearance is heralded by a 'star', the sparkling of the 'stone'. The soul issues forth from the night of initial chaos and finds itself re-established in its original integrity. The inner light and fire are rekindled, and, in the heart, the dark fire is transformed by the living light in harmony with the divine Water and the Woman, the 'Virgin Sophia', 'Celestial Mercury' who opens the 'gate of heaven' that is in the heart. According to Gichtel, this whole transformation amounts to inwardly channeling the 'covetousness' of the 'old man' into desire for God, in such a way that the Virgin Sophia and Holy Spirit coincide with the desire. The man then experiences successive illuminations: the '*black* stone' has become *white*.

Finally, the 'red work' enables one, at the end of the 'Great Coction', to obtain the Philosophers' Stone, which changes metals into gold. The soul experiences definitive illumination, a state in which the opposites fuse: the 'two white doves', the 'birds of Hermes', Sulphur and Mercury, are transformed into a single bird, the 'Phoenix', which sparkles like the sun and attains to heaven; the solar principle regains mastery over the individuality, the man becomes the 'King clothed in purple'.

It is easy to see that the alchemical process unfolds in the same order as all processes of spiritual realization, an order that is perfectly defined in the well-known, classic formula of the 'three ways', purgation, illumination, and union, which correspond analogously to the 'three phases' of the Great Work. Here we have the explanation for the assimilation—possibly surprising to some—of several phenomena, marking the alchemical process, to events in the life of Christ and the Virgin. Thus the commencement of the Work corresponds to the Annunciation; the appearance of the 'white stone' to that of the Child-God, and the sparkling brightness heralding it, to the star of Bethlehem; according to Fulcanelli, this sparkle, or star, shows that the 'philosophical mixture' has been made canonically and announces the birth of the alchemical Child-King. And when the white stone becomes the Philosophers' Stone, the latter is assimilated to Christ. The purpose of these parallels is obviously to make us understand that the true goal of alchemy is of a spiritual order, that it is a way of regeneration for man.

Now, within this alchemical way—and here we rejoin the object of our study—the Virgin Mary has a leading role to play. She performs it, first of all, on the operative plane. Let us recall the words of Fulcanelli, quoted at the beginning of the chapter, to the effect that the *Black Virgins* found in the crypts of churches, the statues of 'Our Lady Underground', represent the matter on which the alchemist is to work, that is, matter buried in principle underground, 'a black substance of stone-like appearance' or, according to an expression found among certain authors, 'the philosophers' earth'.

Before proceeding, let us explain that, in order to be understood, this manner of speaking needs to be placed within the intellectual perspective of the times when alchemy was practiced. In fact, what could be more surprising and scandalous than to say to a twentieth century reader that the Virgin is this dark material, this 'earth' that will need to be purified in order to become the 'subject' of the Great Work, for the proposition could suggest a materialistic reduction of the All-Holy Mother of God to a morsel of common matter, which would be both blasphemous and stupid. This is obviously not the intention. Clearly this manner of speaking belongs to the language of traditional symbolism, which always leads thought in a vertical direction, which is to say that the visible material object points to an intellectual or spiritual reality; it goes from the Lower to the Higher, from the visible to the invisible; never the reverse, which would be a materialistic and reductionist point of view. Having said that, and given that a symbol, in the traditional sense, being neither an allegory nor, even less, a conventional sign, has a real ontological value due to the fact that by analogy it is linked to an invisible reality towards which it points, it is perfectly legitimate to say that some material object 'is' the superior reality that it stands for; plainly it is so in a certain way, which, while not being an identification, is nevertheless very real. We have already given many examples with regard to the Virgin, who is called 'fountain', 'garden', 'tree', 'rose', 'gate', etc., and, precisely, 'earth'. Why then can she not be called the alchemists' 'earth', seeing that in any case alchemy derives from a spiritual activity in which all the 'materials' used in the 'laboratory' really denote principles governing the life of the world and of man? In order to thoroughly understand what the hermetic authors mean when they posit this sort of equation, Black Virgin = alchemist's earth, we need to remember all that was said previously about the three levels of earth symbolism as applied to the Virgin: the metaphysical level, where the word refers to *Materia prima* or *Prakriti*; the cosmological level, where it refers to the substance of the cosmos; and, finally, the properly material level, where it denotes the mineral earth. If so many religious texts have seen fit to praise Mary under this symbol, is this not because it is a particularly evocative image of what the Mother is? The Virgin Mary 'is' the earth in the sense that she incarnates Universal Substance by realizing it in herself, and so likewise she is 'Queen of the World' or, to use Villon's term, the 'Earthly Regent'.

The *Black Virgin* teaches that hidden 'underground', as she is in the crypt, is 'the mineral light', deeper than a 'despised corpse', say the alchemists in speaking of the 'remote matter' of the Work, 'despised but not despicable', which suggests the words of the *Song of Songs*, applied in the Middle Ages to the Black Virgin: *Nigra sum sed formosa*, 'I am black, but beautiful'. For if the earth, our earth, situated at the low-point of the cosmos, can, because of this, appear from a certain point of view as a not very glorious 'element', the least glorious of the four, it is nevertheless what, from another perspective, encloses the vital energies that, born of the heavenly light, cause all vegetable nature to grow. Hidden in darkness, the black statue teaches that in the very depths of her body, she conceals the Light of the world. Because of this, certain of these statues are shown with a radiating sun over the womb. And this is why the Black Virgin is to some degree 'Our Lady of Alchemy', she who presides over the process of the Great Work.

As already mentioned, the moment at which this Great Work commences is compared to the Annunciation, as can be seen, for example, in a scene sculpted on a tympanum of the door of the chapel of Jacques Cœur, studied by E. Canseliet. First, God the Father is seen pointing to the well-known alchemical symbol of the earth, a circle surmounted by a cross, and here representing the 'matter of the Work'. Below this is the archangel greeting Mary with the first four words of the Ave, while the Holy Spirit descends upon her in the form of a dove. The scene should be interpreted in an alchemical sense, so that Mary is the 'earth' or matter of the Work, and the descent of the Holy Spirit the penetration of the Spirit into heavy matter. It goes without saying that the significance of the whole scene is of a spiritual order. As already said, the 'material of the Work' is essentially the individuality of the practitioner, that is to say of common man, who, possessed by his passions and his attachment to material things, is, in the final analysis, a prisoner of his ego. The latter has become *black*, captive to the shadows of sin, but contains, as does the matter of the Work, a kernel of beauty, of light, which must be striven for in order that it emerge from darkness. Having become a hard ore, the ego must be dissolved and reconstituted so as to be able to accede to the life of the Spirit. *Solve et coagula*, the famous formula in fact sums up the essential alchemical operation.

This is a difficult operation, in which the practitioner receives help from the Holy Virgin. *She makes herself black so as to show him the way*; like her, he too needs to become 'earth', the 'Heavenly Earth', Substance, that is to say that which is perfectly 'humble' (*humilis*, like *humus*) and 'docile', the two characteristics of *Materia prima,* as we have seen, which are the indispensable conditions for the activity of the Spirit to be manifested in the practitioner. Man needs to undergo initiatic 'death', that is to say 'forgetfulness of self' in the full sense of this expression, by casting off, with the help of the Virgin, all the dross of the ego. This is the 'black work', after which the mystery of the Annunciation is repeated for him: the Spirit penetrates him and transforms what in him was the 'black virgin', into the 'white virgin', enabling him to pass from the darkness of the earth to the light. The moment the Spirit penetrates, a white portion that is aqueous and airy, mercurial and volatile, separates out, and, in its development, settles on the sulphur and consummates the 'hermetic marriage'.

In sum, *within the alchemical perspective*, the Black Virgin is the prototype to which the individual soul needs to conform; it needs to become 'black virginity', or 'humble earth', that is to say, to 'naught itself' in perfect humility so as to return to the state of *Materia prima*, of virgin matter qualified to receive the influx of the Spirit. Man can only do this with the help of Mary, and this is why the alchemists assigned her such an important place. She is truly the 'Virgo Paritura', she who gives birth to the 'stone' as she gives birth to Christ, which is to say that she brings the soul forth to the light. And the alchemists were not the only ones who understood this; the Christian people also felt—no doubt to a lesser degree—that the *Black Virgin is the initiating Virgin, who through light causes death and resurrection. Her black color signifies that she penetrates the darkness for man and thereby admits him to the Light.*

We saw above that the primary matter of the Work has to lose its hardness, be purified, and, for this to take place, to suffer a dissolution. The dissolving agent is 'philosophical mercury.' And here again we find the Virgin, not under the aspect of 'earth', but of 'water', which is related to mercury as solvent. This is why the 'Sealed Fountain'—a Marian title—which is also the *Fons Vitae* and the *Fons juventutis*, symbolizes mercury. In his *Philosophie naturelle des métaux*, Le Trévisan, an hermetic author, describes this stream of living water of volatile essence, this potent solvent able to penetrate all metals, in particular gold, and, with the help of the dissolved substances, accomplish the entire Great Work. Alchemists say that the Virgin 'is' this Water and this Mercury. Grillot de Givry writes that 'Mary is the *aqua permanens*, the *aqua albificans* of the Spagyrics';

she is the 'spiritual mercury' of life, the 'virginal milk' of the 'chemical philosophers', and he quotes the following lines from Van Helpen's *L'Escalier des Sages*: 'Spiritual Mercury is a principle of life for all creatures; it is the receptacle of spiritual Sulphur (Christ), which, proceeding from the general source of Light, comes to settle in the womb of that universal spirit called mercury (the *materia purissima* of Mary), impregnating it with every sort of form.' Here we must remember that it is a question of spiritual mercury, of which common mercury is simply the material symbol in the mineral kingdom, but a true symbol, so that the qualities of spiritual mercury are to be found therein, to an inferior degree, certainly, corresponding to the material plane, but rendering this plane, within the spiritual perspective of alchemy, permeable to the activity of celestial mercury. And so, within the alchemical operation, at both its levels, we are justified in assimilating the Virgin to mercury in a certain way, just as, within the same perspective, she was assimilated to 'earth'. In passing, let us remark that the astrological sign of the Virgin, which we have discussed in previous chapters, is the 'point of exaltation' of the planet Mercury, a connection the alchemists take into account in their calendar. This sort of 'kinship' of the Virgin with the element in question is explained by the fact that, while spiritual Mercury is the virginal element, it is yet fecundating, the generator of things, determining all the developmental phases of substances, producing cohesion, determining affinities, in both the intellectual and physical orders, fertilizing the seeds in the earth and the Great Work in the athanor. At the cosmic level, it is the *spiritus vitae*, 'the soul of life' or 'the soul of things', the mediator through which creative activity takes place, 'the water of life', the subtle fluid directing all the phenomena produced in the world. At the supreme level, it is the spiritualizing 'Celestial Soul', which is none other than the 'Celestial Woman' who governs all things; in short, it is the metaphysical principle we invariably return to, *Materia prima—Prakriti*, according to its mythological name—which, once fertilized by the active divine Principle, becomes the generator of life at every level, and with which Mary is identified as her eternal archetype. This is why the Virgin presides over this principle of life in the universe, as warden of secondary causes and primordial energies.

Grillot de Givry writes further that in order to create the 'Philosophers' Stone', it is necessary to possess that which bore the Spirit in Genesis. Mary is thus revealed as the 'proximate matter' of the Philosophers' Stone: she is the 'mercurial water' and principle of things, the 'hermetical Moon' of the Spagyrics, by means of which the condensation of the Rouah Elohim in the *corpus glorificatum* is effected (here let us recall that the name Mariam synthesizes the creative act of the Spirit; *Rouah* brooding over the primordial Waters, *Maim*). According to the same author,

> This explains why the sixteenth century alchemists held their assemblies in the basilica of Notre Dame in Paris, under the immediate protection of the immaculate Virgin.

From the spiritual point of view, Mary, as celestial Mercury, is the 'solvent' capable of dissolving the hardness of the ego—just as the 'remote matter' of the Work, in order to be purified, is submitted to a 'mercury bath'—thus freeing the 'mercury' in it and rendering it fit to receive and unite with the fire of Sulphur, so as to realize the 'hermetic marriage' and give birth to the new man.

The allusion just made to the church of Notre Dame quite naturally leads to the question of the relationships of alchemy and the Virgin to the construction and function of churches. These relationships are particularly noticeable and important at Notre Dame in Paris, which, because of this, has been called the 'alchemical cathedral'. Thus, on the pier at the north entrance of the west side we see a statue of the Virgin surrounded by the signs of the zodiac. E. Canseliet, who has made a close study of this church, says that by having this figure sculpted, Bishop William wished to show the 'student' that the 'matter of the Work' was the 'Great Lady', the inhabitant of the place and ever Virgin Mother of the divine Son of Man.

To be sure, alchemical signs and symbols are to be found in many other religious buildings, especially those where a black statue of the Virgin is venerated, as at Chartres, but without necessarily excluding those where no statue is found, for example at Amiens and, precisely, Notre Dame at Paris! The Black Virgin of Paris in fact has her seat elsewhere, as was mentioned in chapter one. Moreover, what we are going to say about churches dedicated to the Virgin can be applied, *mutatis mutandis*, to all old churches constructed according to canonical and traditional rules.

An interesting building for understanding these connections between alchemy and the Christian temple is the Breton basilica of Notre Dame de Bon-Secours, at Guingamp, which shelters a black statue of the Virgin, the object of a famous summer pilgrimage; this building was studied by H. Blanquet in a special edition of the magazine *Atlantis* (no. 253, in 1969). While the study contains a certain number of hazardous and frankly unacceptable extrapolations that are, besides, somewhat beyond the scope of our subject, the core nevertheless offers much that is worth remembering about this 'hermetic basilica', as the author calls it, and the analysis of the alchemical itinerary that can be detected in the building, according to him, appears on examination altogether serious and worthy of attention.

The chapel of the Black Virgin is entered by the north door of the building. According to the author, the statue is placed on a pedestal in the form of a baphomet. Inscribed on the ground is a labyrinth, which is a reduced version of the one at Chartres and which, very interestingly, has at its center a *black stone* on which the words *Ave Maria* are carved in white! It could hardly be more explicit! The great interest of these two elements can be seen immediately, although not mentioned by H. Blanquart. First, the labyrinth itself, which is often encountered in churches dedicated to the Virgin, especially those with a black statue, and which is directly related to initiation. Indeed, the walking of the labyrinth by the faithful is one of the forms of the 'descent into hell', that is to say, of the descent into the obscure parts of the individuality in order to take cognizance of those elements of the being that constitute obstacles on the path of spiritual realization with a view to rectifying and overcoming them. The meanders of the labyrinth symbolize the difficult detours required by such an introspection, which, however, enables one, at the end of the journey, to reach the center of the being whence spiritual ascension can be effected. In a more 'outward' and well-known sense, the walking of the labyrinth is a substitute for pilgrimage; which amounts to the same thing, for pilgrimage is a form of 'journey to the center'; and it is worth noting that wherever an important church is dedicated to the Virgin, black or not, there is always a pilgrimage, as is the case at Guingamp. Returning to the labyrinth found there, its center is especially remarkable in that it consists of a black stone, which leads us directly back to alchemy. We immediately think of the famous hermetic cryptogramme VITRIOL, referring to the first phase of the Work and composed of the first letters of the following words: *Visita interiora terrae, rectificando invenies occultam lapidem*, 'Visit the interior of the earth, through rectification [that is to say, through purification] you will find the hidden stone,' the 'matter of the Work'. And here, at Guingamp, this stone is explicitly assimilated to the Virgin—*Ave Maria*—and refers to her role, which we discussed earlier.

The sides of the chapel depict the twelve apostles and, sculpted in circles at their feet, the alchemical metals, as on the sarcophagus of the Virgin at the north portal of Notre Dame in Paris. Thus the 'matter of the Work' is again represented. The presence of the twelve Apostles here signifies the relationship of the metals to the signs of the zodiac, and indeed we know that the correlation of the apostles with the twelve signs of the zodiac is traditional in Christian symbolism. And by way of confirmation, outside the building, to the south and west, we find a profusion of St James' cockleshells connected to the south to a no longer extant chapel dedicated to this saint, the patron of hermeticists. Moreover, when we enter by the north portal of the transept, we encounter the 'Chapel of the Dead' with an altar made of *black and grey stones*; the stained glass window situated above the portal is likewise of the same black and grey shades. All these elements are sufficiently revealing: we have before us an evocation of the first phase of the alchemical process, the 'black work', which, as already said, is symbolically related to a death, death, in the Christian tradition, being linked to the cardinal direction of north.

On the south side of the church was a stained glass window—gone today, but known to us from an illustration—the alchemical significance of which was clear enough: the upper section depicted the celestial Virgin bathed in the sun and ascending in the triangle of the Divinity. In hermetic symbolism, this representation of the Assumption corresponds to the taking flight of the 'matter' spiritualized by the light of Christ. The *Black Virgin* has become the *White Virgin*; this is the second phase of the Work. It will have been noticed that the Virgin wears a *blue* mantle and a *violet* gown; these two colors are significant and relate to the unfolding of the alchemical process. In hermeticism, blue is regarded as an attenuated black, while violet is a mixture of blue and red, and so, according to our author, the garment symbolizes the intermediate stage between the 'black work' and the 'red work'. In our opinion, however, caution should be exercised accepting this conclusion, for it seems the problem of the exact colors of the garments of authentic original Black Virgins has yet to be fully clarified. Far more certain is the meaning of the garments in the icon of Cambrai where the Virgin wears a black mantle over a red gown, that is to say, the colors of the garments of Isis in Apuleus.

The 'red work', the end of the process, is represented to the west, by a predominantly red stained glass window depicting Pentecost, with the Virgin wearing a red gown beneath the blue mantle. Let us observe in passing that this representation of the phases of the Great Work in the colors of the stained glass is not confined to Guingamp; it is found in numerous cathedrals, in the three rose-windows of the north, south, and west.

To conclude our remarks on Blanquart's study, let us note that the author points to a number of facts proving that the entire territory around the basilica and the site of Guingamp was strongly marked by hermeticism. Outside the town, at the church of Notre Dame de la Cour, we find an alchemical stained glass window showing the Virgin clothed in a blue mantle, a white gown and a red tunic, the three colors of the 'Work'. In the church of Bourbriac is another alchemical stained glass window, again in the northern part, showing, from bottom to top, the five-pointed star related to the 'white work', the alchemical vase, and the *Rosa mystica*, the Marian symbol we have already studied, which is known as the 'philosophers' flower' because it evokes the idea of resurrection. This meaning is particularly clear in the figure of the rose placed in the center of the Cross, for the Cross represents the initiatic death that makes possible the blossoming of the rose, the sign of the resurrection.

If all churches dedicated to the Black Virgin do not present as developed an alchemical imagery as that at Guingamp, they nevertheless play an altogether similar role to that of alchemy, which, precisely, explains the presence of hermetic symbols when found in them. Let us add that this is equally true of all regularly constructed churches.

To begin with, let us consider the first case, that of buildings where the Black Virgin is to be found. These are generally built at sites where we find reminders of the Celtic Age in the form of megaliths. This is particularly true of the Auvergne. Bonvin has succeeded in showing that at the center of the Auvergne are three principal logan-stones, Combroude, Billon, and Orcival, which determine three series of concentric circles upon which numerous Black Virgins of this region are situated. The expansion of this schema has enabled him to relate all the Virgins of the Auvergne to a 'point of origin' at which a logan-stone or an important megalithic center is to be found. Louis Charpentier arrived at a similar conclusion for the site of Chartres, which one can read about in his *The Mysteries of Chartres Cathedral*.

The connection with megaliths leads to the question of telluric currents. These currents of energy can be positive and beneficial or negative and dangerous; in the latter case, they have been known to render an area infertile. The presence of cosmic or celestial currents at a place renders it beneficial and, in the past, it was for that reason marked by a menhir or dolmen, both of which served, along with logan-stones, to channel and augment these natural forces and neutralize negative ones. The upright stone condenses the energy while the dolmen recreates the cavern, or grotto, where one seeks what is called the 'gift of the earth'.

The cathedral of Chartres is built on a knoll where the currents of energy are exceptionally strong. On the mound where the building was constructed there is a sacred stone called the 'stone of Belisama', the Celtic Great Mother whose name has been mentioned more than once. The church is built over this stone, and, according to L. Charpentier, functions as a dolmen: it is placed over the Druidic grotto which is situated 'under the altar of the idols', to quote a sixteenth century witness. The grotto is the 'dolmenic chamber', where a very powerful telluric current is manifested, such that the crypt of Chartres is a veritable 'sounding box' for this telluric energy.

These currents of energy are the manifestation of what in bygone days was called the 'wouivre', that is, the serpent (Latin *vipera*), to which this great current of subterranean life—the chthonic aspect of Universal Energy, the *spiritus mundi*, the 'Soul of the World'—is compared. This takes us back to alchemy, for, as we have seen, the goal of the latter is to gather, concentrate, and stabilize the vital current, the Mercury, which, when condensed in the 'Stone', allows the evolution of the initial 'material/matter' to accelerate.

This current, however, ceaselessly acts upon all things, including man, and the places where it is concentrated offer man a powerful means of 'mutation'. Now why, as at Chartres, were old churches so often built on sites where pagan sanctuaries had previously stood? This is because traditional churches were the work of builders who possessed the same geo-biological knowledge—as we would say today—as those of the previous civilization, who further knew that a church should be something far more than a simple 'place of assembly' of the faithful, as is claimed today by a whole clergy that no longer knows anything of important matters. A church was conceived as a tool for capturing the energies of a place, specially chosen for its 'virtues'. The currents, welling up from the earth in the crypt, and there concentrated, rose to the vault, which, resting on the pillars, acted as the roof of the dolmen, functioning as a paraboloid reflector; there they mixed with the cosmic currents coming from heaven. In this way the *earth*, under the influence of *heaven*, gave birth in this place to a special active radiation which furthermore was boosted by the shapes and dimensions of a building constructed according to the rules of numerology and sacred geometry, which was dealt with in our book *Le symbolisme du temple chrétien* and the recent excellent study by Jacques Thomas, *La divine proportion et l'art de geometrie* (1993).

In churches that are constructed as they ought to be, on appropriate sites, *something* penetrates us, *something* floods us on entering, and the nearer we approach the crossing of the transept the stronger the enchantment: the maximum is attained at the point of intersection of the axes of the nave and transept, or near it, *where normally the altar would be built in order to benefit most from the radiation.*

Now, herein lies the importance: an individual who enters Chartres, for example, is bathed in cosmo-telluric effluvia that act both upon him and the rites performed there. In fact, in penetrating him, the energies of which we speak attune him to the cosmos, making him feel that he vibrates with the entire world, for he comes into contact with the principles regulating his and all life, and these so to speak force him, to go beyond the limits of his ego, thereby preparing him to receive the heavenly influx vehicled by the rites—at least when these are performed properly, a detail, unfortunately, that needs to be added these days! Thus the famous pilgrimages to the sanctuaries of the Virgin constituted spiritual and energy 'cures.' And something similar happened in the grottoes where the 'Mothers' who preceded Our Lady, such as Belisama, carried out their initiations.

These energies that penetrate the faithful in the churches under consideration strongly resemble the alchemists' 'mercurial bath' that serves to purify the 'matter'. From this perspective, the church can be compared to the alchemical laboratory and to what transpires therein. The crypt is the place where something like the 'black work' is performed, the 'descent into hell' (*interiora terrae*); the nave is where the 'white work' and 'red work' are accomplished, under the influence of 'mercury' (the telluric currents), and 'sulphur' (the heavenly influx vehicled by the rites of the sacred work). With regard to this last idea, we believe it advisable to alert the reader to the attitude of many authors who address these subjects and confuse, or seem to confuse, cosmological and spiritual realities. This is particularly true of those attached to the New Age Movement, but this state of mind is also encountered among those whose names we have cited for their often very interesting and useful information about Black Virgins and churches, but all of whose outlooks we nevertheless do not share.

Thus, when speaking of the Virgin, too many authors seem to see in her no more than an allegorical 'figure' of Mercury, of the universal Fluid, whereas in her capacity as 'Queen of the World' her role is rather that of regent of this Fluid. When she is assimilated to Mercury and the universal Fluid, something we ourselves have done, it is according to the mode of traditional symbolic thought explained earlier. Now, this role of 'cosmic regent' is represented by the widely known image of Mary with the serpent under her feet, with the usual interpretation given to this image being that of victory over Satan. This meaning is altogether true, since it is founded upon a passage from Genesis (3:14–15), but it possesses another meaning that is neither alien to the first nor contradictory: Mary is the regent of all cosmic forces—symbolized by the serpent—and directs them beneficially, whereas Satan, who is able to act upon them in a certain way, naturally does so in a malignant sense. This is certainly not a personal opinion, for this meaning also exists, but in a hidden way, in Genesis with regard to *Nahash*—a complex topic we cannot address here. In any event, what should be said regarding the meaning of this image of the Virgin is that it refers to the essential role played by Mary vis-à-vis the man engaged on the spiritual path, during the stage we shall call in alchemical terms the 'black work', or, according to another way of speaking, the 'descent into hell'. This is in fact a dangerous stage, because of the meeting on the way with forces that can take a dark turn, which is when Satan acts. Man has need of a guide on this route, and the best of guides is Mary, the directress of all vital forces.

In this way, the Virgin Mary appears as the great mediator of all spiritual realization, the mechanics of which alchemical language makes understandable. Now, spiritual realization is a re-creation, and all re-creation needs to be effected on the model of the original Creation, through the harmonious union of Spirit and Water, that is to say, in mankind's case, of the masculine and feminine, *animus* and *anima*, which alchemy refers to as 'sulphur' and 'mercury'—a harmonious union, we have said, for in fact harmony is nonexistent with the average man. It is thus a question of 'dissolving' the chaotic 'matter' of the individual, of 'dissociating' it in order to recompose it in a better state. The Virgin, insofar as she embodies 'Celestial Mercury', enables the 'mercury' in man to be released, freeing it in order to unite it to the spiritual 'sulphur' following the transcendent model of the Incarnation, the sublime mystery in which Mary is shown as the all pure Substance to which the Word is united.

The way in which this regeneration is realized is clarified in the pages of Titus Burckhardt's work dealing with the definition and methods of spiritual alchemy. He shows how the chaotic and opaque human soul, if it is to be filled with heavenly light, must become ordered and 'crystalline'. The soul, he says, is congealed in a state of sterile hardness and needs to be subjected to the purifications imposed upon the alchemical 'matter': first 'liquefy' and then re-'congeal' it in order to rid it of its impurities, then make it undergo 'fusion' and, finally, 'crystallization'. The change is effected through an actualization and co-ordination of the forces of the soul, which correspond analogically to the hot, cold, dry, and wet forces of nature. In the soul, the hot corresponds to the expansive force, the source of joy and happiness; the cold to the force of contraction, the source of fear and withdrawal into oneself; the wet to the force of the 'liquefying' passivity of the soul; the dry to the force of the 'stabilizing' activity of the spirit. And these four forces are attached to our two well-known complementary principles, Sulphur and Mercury, the igneous and stabilizing qualities to the active pole of Sulphur, and the contracting and solvent qualities to the passive pole of Mercury. In other words, Sulphur corresponds to the masculine, the *yang*, the active, expansive principle attached to the spirit, whereas Mercury corresponds to the feminine, the *yin*, the passive, receptive principle attached to substance, to the vital forces, the principle of plasticity, source of beauty, goodness, tenderness, compassion, and intuition.

The state of man depends on the combination of these principles and qualities. 'Hardness' of soul comes from the alliance of the 'dry', stabilizing quality of the mind, with the 'cold', contracting quality of the parallel state of soul; 'dissipation' comes from the association of the 'warm', expansive force of 'desire', with the 'moist', dissolving power of the passive state of soul. We have here two states of disequilibrium and disharmony, to which others could be added.

The harmonious balance of the soul results from the alternation of expansion and contraction comparable to that of breathing and of the marriage of the 'stabilizing' activity of the spirit with the 'liquid' receptivity of the soul, according to T. Burckhardt, and is realized if the powers of the soul are not permitted to be determined by external impulses, but respond instead to spiritual activity. As this activity needs to be 'centered on the heart', the spiritual means best adapted to this end is the repetition of a verbal symbol, the invocation of a divine Name. The phases of interior alchemy, the successive liquefactions and crystallizations, appear as a permutation of the sacred symbol within the soul, in conformity with the divine realities it expresses. In the act of invocation the three aspects constituting the spiritual way are realized: doctrinal truth, which is addressed to the metaphysical in man; volitive virtue and concentration, which aim to 'dissolve' the knot of egocentrism, the obstacle to contemplation; and, finally, spiritual alchemy which, in conveying the radiation of the Grace present in the divine symbol, transforms the psycho-physical structure of the individual by acting upon the organic layers of consciousness.

If we have spent some time on this somewhat difficult description of spiritual alchemy (which, in the final analysis, is none other than a particular form of the spiritual way in general and the explanation it gives of the way), this is to throw more light on the role played therein by the Virgin Mary. As will have been gathered, the Virgin, both as celestial Woman and by means of her function as 'celestial Mercury', is for everyone that perfect *anima* that extricates the *animus* and *anima* from the vein-stone in which sin has enclosed them as a chaotic whole, with a view to their harmonious union. This beneficial action of the Mother of God can be accomplished in two ways: through the invocation of her Name, as mentioned above, to which we shall shortly return, but also through the veneration, or better, contemplation of her holy image, which corresponds directly to what could have been—and can be—a pilgrimage to the Virgin and especially the Black Virgin.

In our book *Mythes, rites et symbols,* we spoke about the nature and function of the icon as a tool of contemplation, in the manner of a *mandala*; we say specifically 'of the icon', for the latter is not simply any 'religious' image, but in reality a 'sacred' image, that is to say, conceived and executed according to precise rules, and, because of this, able to 'open' the invisible world to the view of the one who contemplates it. Such is the case with the icon of Our Lady of Czestochowa (see Plate XXXI) the analysis of which, done some time ago in 1940 by F. Schuon in an article in *Études traditionnelles,* explains very well what we mean. This black image, as, of course, all others of the same type, yields a veritable metaphysical teaching. The dark color of the Virgin refers to Divine Non-manifestation of which she, as Mother of the Word, who is Himself also a manifestation of the Non-manifested, is the support. She represents the substantial condition for the manifestation of the Word, its base; as such, she is to support the 'Unique', and not be stained by the 'Multiple', symbolically identified with 'the flesh', the realm of quantity and differentiation. The image thus becomes a tool of contemplation: the soul of the contemplative is, like Mary, to realize the birth of the Word in its heart, and for that, it needs, like Her, to be 'pure' and 'empty' so as to serve as support to the divine Presence. 'If your soul is serving and pure like Mary,' says Angelus Silesius, 'it should instantly be pregnant with God.' Like the Virgin, it should bear the imprint of Non-manifestation, that is to say 'obscurity'. This imprint is, transitorily and secondarily, the *nox profunda* and the 'descent into hell', which constitutes the 'initiatic death' of which we have spoken and which is expressed hermetically as the 'black work'; permanently, it is 'extinction' or 'indifference' with regard to 'the world', that is to 'illusion', the state of 'poverty in spirit' and 'humility'. The color black then signifies 'silence' or absence of manifestation in the soul of the contemplative, the *hesychia* of Eastern spirituality that F. Schuon, in another study, likens to *nirvana*.

Such, in the final analysis, was the role of the black images of Mary. To all who contemplated them with a profound devotion, they offered the means of transforming themselves—to different degrees and each according to his possibilities, for, obviously, we do not claim that all thereby attained perfect 'poverty in spirit'; it should even be said that of such there was without doubt but a small minority; but all, we repeat, provided they had the right intention, would have found there a means of effecting a change in their life. But let it be clearly understood that we do not claim that only the black statues or images of the Virgin fulfilled such a function, which would be ridiculous. Quite simply, what needs to be said is that the black image, perhaps because of its fascination, was better adapted to provoke in the soul of the faithful a shock calculated to bring about a conversion.

Let us return to the other spiritual means mentioned above, the invocation of the Name, which, according to T. Burckhardt's explanation, is calculated to bring about the alchemical transformation of man. In the first place, it is obviously a matter of the Divine Name, which, for the Christian, is the Name of Jesus, the repetition of which, whether or not synchronized with the breath, constitutes the 'Prayer of the Heart' of Byzantine spirituality, the practice of which also exists in Occidental spirituality, as J. Borella has shown in his discussion of the manual of L. Lanau, *De la deification des justes* (1993). Now the Name of Mary plays a similar role, which explains its association with the name of Jesus. The practice of the 'Prayer of the Heart' includes, along with the invocation 'Lord, Jesus Christ, Son of God, have mercy on me,' the invocation 'Most Holy Mother of God, my Sovereign, have mercy on me,' but in a smaller proportion. We are faced with an altogether similar situation in the Western Church with the recitation of the Rosary, which F. Schuon has quite rightly called the 'Prayer of the Heart' of the West. Concerning this topic, we shall refer again to the study of the Rosary in our book cited a little earlier apropos the icon, recalling only the essentials here.

As repetitive prayer, the recitation of the Rosary falls into the category of incantation, the aim of which is to bring the subject to a different state of consciousness from that of ordinary life. The repetition of the Divine Name actualizes the 'remembrance of God' in the mind and establishes it in the heart, which is thereby transformed. The Rosary invokes two Divine Names, Jesus and Mary (for, as we have seen, the name of Mary is also a Divine Name), and it is in these two Names that the operative force of this prayer resides. In reciting the *Ave*, the person praying contemplates the mystery of the Incarnation, but, not content to consider it simply as an external reality, he lives it on his own behalf, for this mystery is, in fact, the mystery of the reintegration of fallen man. Now, in order to be reintegrated, to recover his archetype, that is to say 'what he is' from all eternity in the Word, *he must live the 'mystery of the Virgin' on his own account*; in thought he must identify with the Virgin of the Annunciation and himself be the recipient of Angel's words, greeting him as 'Mary'. The incantation produced by the repetition of the *Name of Mary* enshrined in the words of the Angel, acts upon the 'hardness' of the soul, 'dissolving' and 'liquefying' it, and reducing it to a state of ontological plasticity; a transformation takes place which gradually leads the soul towards the 'virginal' state, thus rendering it fit to receive, with the *Name of Jesus*, the birth of the Word within itself.

We thus see that, lived profoundly, the recitation of the Rosary truly constitutes an instrument of spiritual realization, which is further proved by the invitation of the Church to accompany it with meditation on the 'Joyful, Sorrowful and Glorious Mysteries', which are stages in the life of Mary and should be in the life of the Christian: reception of the Word, birth of Christ in his heart, painful ordeals even as far as the Cross, where the 'old man' is to die, then resurrection and assumption in which he is raised, like Mary, towards the heavenly state, his soul becoming once again 'that which it is from all eternity.' Concerning the subject of the fifteen Mysteries of the Rosary, we have very briefly summarized the commentaries on them given by Fr Chenique in his excellent work dedicated to Mary, *Le Buisson ardent* (1972).

Thus, by recalling that the redemption of man could not have happened on the universal plane, except through the restoration of primordial humanity in the intimate union of the Virgin and Christ, we return, in ending this chapter, to matters we were considering at the end of the last concerning the Marian Mystery—subject of our whole inquiry. Now, what has just been said regarding the practice of the Rosary, coming as it does at the end of a whole exposition on the alchemical role of the Virgin, and especially the Black Virgin, shows that the same applies on the individual plane, where in every way Mary is she who gives birth to man as 'son of God'. The adage *Ad Jesum per Mariam* bears witness to this, as does the experience of numerous saints for whom the spiritual path was the perpetual inner recitation of the words 'Jesus-Mary'. In spiritual alchemy, these words operate as the 'Sulphur' of the heavenly Fire and the 'Mercury' of the heavenly Water; they constitute a double invocation that can be looked upon, within the perspective in question, as the ritual expression of the primordial androgyne.

It can be seen, then, that the Marian Mystery concerns the whole life of man from the moment his life is to be integrated into an authentic spiritual quest. We are about to discover that this mystery is involved in a sphere not usually associated with it, although such involvement follows from everything we have just said.

5

Woman

OUR INTENTION in this final chapter is to throw light on the spiritual role that the Virgin is called upon to play in the relationships between man and woman, particularly in marriage. We believe that no one who has followed the thread of ideas expounded in the previous chapters will be astonished to find Mary in this role, for it follows directly from what has been said about the personality of the Virgin inasmuch as she is the realization par excellence of Woman, she whom the Angel greeted as 'blessed (that is, glorified) among all women'. Furthermore, the pages that follow merely serve to expand—focusing on marriage this time—the themes of spiritual alchemy involving the just dealt with relationships of the *animus* and *anima*.

Besides, the question of the relationships between man and woman, of love, sexuality, and marriage, which is of the utmost importance, as much by the place it occupies in the life and soul of individuals as by its consequences for society, has been for a long time, and continues to be, ill-conceived and badly posed in the Christian world.

For centuries, views on sexuality and the purpose of marriage have been poisoned by an enormous and calamitous misunderstanding about their very nature, a misunderstanding resulting from an exaggerated emphasis on the 'sins of the flesh', and this in turn has fostered a misogyny that tends to view woman as the instrument of sin, or even of the Devil. This misunderstanding does not emanate from certain over-zealous ascetics; it comes to us directly from the greatest teachers. At least in the West, it is always attributed to St Augustine, and not without reason. But it would be wrong to forget that the source is yet more illustrious, for it is the

Apostle Paul who wrote to the Christians at Corinth,

> It is good for a man not to touch a woman. Nevertheless to avoid fornication, let every man have his own wife, and let every woman have her own husband . . . [as for the unmarried] if they cannot contain, let them marry: for it is better to marry than to burn' (1 Cor. 7:1–9).

In this perspective, marriage is, so to say, no more than a last resort: since the physical union of man and woman in the fallen human state is considered bad in itself, and therefore in itself a sin; marriage, which is proposed as a remedy for lust, is in a way degraded to the level of a 'permitted sin'. But to view sexual union as something more or less shameful, far from being a remedy for concupiscence, has only served to exacerbate it, enclosing generations of Christians in a veritable carnal prison that has in many cases compromised the healthy development not only of their earthly existence but, more importantly, of their spiritual life. It is impossible to exaggerate the number of dramas and catastrophes for which such a conception of the relations between man and woman has been responsible.

Yet, in all traditions, love and marriage have been ranked among the most sacred of realities. Thus, in ancient Greece—where however, the practice of love knew grave deviations—marriage, *gamos*, was not only a religious institution, but was even considered and celebrated as a 'mystery', in the Greek sense, that is to say an 'initiation', a *telos*, a *telete*. Dionysios the Areopagite even wrote, 'The Athenians called marriage *telos*, for it is what crowns man for life', which means it 'completes' or 'perfects' the human being, and this is the meaning of the verb *telein* whence *telos* derives. We may judge the matter from the description of the rites that took place in the name of Zeus and Hera, the principal couple, and Artemis, the virgin goddess, in the month of *gamelion*, which is already significant, since this word means 'month of marriages'. The liturgy unfolded in two essential activities: first, a sacrifice to Zeus Teleios at the home of the young man and to Hera Teleia at that of the young woman, followed by the consecration of the woman to Artemis; then the purification of the betrothed couple by means of a bath, the water for which was fetched from the sacred spring Callirhoe. Ch. Picard has shown that the bath was definitely related to the Eleusinian purificatory rites, as the examination of figured monuments proves. This bath assumes particular importance if judged by the fact that, in the wedding procession leading her to the home of the groom, the young woman, who was veiled in white, solemnly carried the *loutrophoros*, the vessel that served for the ritual bath. A ritual fundamentally similar to that of the Greeks was practiced at Rome.

In India, the union of man and woman is ranked as a 'great rite' (*vajna*), equivalent to that of the sacrifice of *soma*, and is celebrated by Brahman officiants. In the marriage pavilion, the bridegroom promises the young woman to ensure her piety, wealth, and pleasure, and, according to a formula from the *Rig-Veda* (x, 85, 36), 'to form but one being with her,' a solemn promise of union in perpetuity. The husband will repeat this formula in the intimacy of the home, at the first coming together of the couple: 'United are our souls, united our hearts, united our bodies. I give my pledge to love you; may it be indissoluble.' After various rites performed near the 'nuptial fire', around which the couple has circled many times, the young man pronounces the formula of marriage. Taken from the *Brhadaranyaka Upanishad* (6, 4, 20–22), this very beautiful formula expresses the rootedness of conjugal union in the divine order, denoted symbolically by Heaven and Earth, of which the two betrothed are the images. Heaven and Earth here indicate *Purusha* and *Prakriti*, and we note in passing that with Zeus and Hera we have seen a certain equivalent in ancient Greek marriage. The formula is as follows:

> I am He, you are She; you are She, I am He; I am Heaven, you are the Earth.... Come, we are going to marry each other.

As they embrace, the husband will repeat the formula in the following form:

> As the Earth welcomes the Fire in its womb, as Heaven encloses Indra in its bosom ... thus I place in you the seed of (N: the name of the son or daughter they desire).

This sacred character of the conjugal act, which, as we have seen, is related to a celestial prototype, is marked in a similar way in Islam, which also possesses a 'ritual of union': as the husband unites with his wife, he pronounces the formula: *bismillah ar-rahman ar-rahim*, 'In the Name of God the Infinitely Good, the All-Merciful.'

In Judaism, too, the sacred character of marriage is strongly underlined, for each marriage is considered as the image of the union of God with His Shekhina. We shall have occasion to return to this.

Pages could be written detailing parallel conceptions belonging to the most diverse traditional cultures. Should we conclude from this that Christianity alone has, as one says, cast 'Noah's Mantle' over marriage and sexuality, and that this is its authentic way of looking at things? Evidently not, and we do well to refuse as its authentic teaching what has only been a betrayal of it. In fact, how is it possible to admit that Divine Revelation could offer man an aberration such as the one we have called to mind?

In order to know the true Christian teaching in this sphere, we have only to re-open the Epistles of St Paul himself at the passages which squarely contradict the one quoted earlier, for this latter merely represents the personal opinion of the Apostle, whereas elsewhere he transmits the teaching of Christ, which has a very different tone. The essential text is Ephesians 5:22–32:

> For the husband is the head of the wife, even as Christ is the head of the Church: and he is the savior of the body. . . . Husbands, love your wives, even as Christ also loved the Church. . . . So ought men to love their wives as their own bodies. He that loveth his wife, loveth himself. . . .';

and, quoting Genesis, he writes,

> For this cause shall a man leave his father and mother, and shall be joined unto his wife, and they two shall be one flesh' (As is often the case in the Scriptures, the word 'flesh' means, 'living being').

After which he writes these essential words: 'This is a great mystery; but I speak concerning Christ and the Church.'

A 'mystery'; once again the word refers to initiation, to *telos*, as Dionysios the Areopagite said. It is true that the meaning of this teaching is not immediately clear and must be explained in the context of Judeo-Christian thought and modes of expression. This, however, will be all the more easily done after we have first considered the problem of love from the universal perspective, that is to say, by recalling in broad outline the metaphysics of union.

The ultimate meaning of love, of *eros*, 'desire', was definitively pointed out by Plato in the *Symposium* (205D–206A), where his mouth-piece, Diotima, defines its essence as the desire for possession of the supreme Good, that is to say God. The physical impulse of *eros*, in fact, is the last degree of a superior impulse that seeks to induce man to abandon duality and the state of separation attendant upon the current fallen status of humanity, so as to rejoin Unity. This is to say that *eros* has its source in God himself, whence its sacred character. And it is in God that the ideal relationship between man and woman should first be considered: it is to be deduced from the Divine Bi-Unity constituted, as we have seen, from the Eternal Masculine and the Eternal Feminine, the Active and Passive, as characteristics of the creative Essence and Substance, or Universal Nature, the two corresponding respectively, at the supreme degree of Beyond-Being, to the Absolute, or Transcendence, and the Infinite, or Universal Possibility. Ibn-Arabi gives a good exposition of this doctrine in *The Wisdom of the Prophets*, writing that 'women are like the passive receptacle of the act of man', and are situated in relation to him as

Universal Nature (*at-tabiah*) to God; it is truly in Universal Nature that God causes the forms of the world to come to light by means of the projection of His Will and through the Divine Act, which is manifested as sexual in the world of forms constituted by the elements (that is to say the material world).

This doctrine leads directly to the idea of the androgyne as prototype of man (in the sense of *homo*, that is to say *vir* and *mulier*). The androgyne is properly the image of God in man, an image constituted by specific human characteristics, which are reflections of Divine Qualities and Attributes. These latter, relate in turn to the two aspects of God, who is Masculine in His Transcendence and Feminine in His Infinity, whence the specific characteristics of man and woman are deduced, characteristics that at first sight appear opposed, but which in reality are clearly complementary. Within this perspective it can be said that man is opposed to woman as expansive, creative active energy is opposed to receptive passive energy; as outwardness is opposed to inwardness. Man, says Paul Evdokimov, is ec-static, woman en-static; man projects himself outwards to master the world, woman turns towards her being; she is not action, but being; again, they are opposed as 'majesty' against 'beauty', strength against tenderness and love, rigor against mercy, goodness, compassion, and sacrifice; as reason and judgment against intuition, objectivity against subjectivity and feeling; as proximity of the spirit against proximity of Nature (Maya) and Wisdom, but all of these oppositions are nicely summed up in the pair *animus-anima*.

In the present state of Creation, the problem is that the human being is not yet really *born*, that is to say, his characteristic traits enjoy no harmonious equilibrium, and, precisely because of this, seem opposed and engender conflicts. In fact, the male human being possesses in himself what has been called the 'inner woman'—designated by the term *anima*—that is to say a collection of traits proper to the feminine being. These traits, however, only exist in him in a virtual state and must be actualized if the complete and harmonious human state is to be realized. And, from her side, the female human being possesses, also in a virtual state, traits proper to the male, an *animus*, which needs to undergo the same treatment. Now, it is here that *eros*, love, intervenes, bringing together the two beings and effecting an exchange of complementary qualities. When love is what it should be, it makes it possible for each to realize the integration of the *animus* or *anima*, as the case might be: woman enables man to actualize his *anima*, his 'inner woman', and man enables woman to actualize her potential virility. If the synthesis is successful, the beings recover the androgynous state and the principial androgyne is then hypostasized in the united couple.

We recognize in this description the alchemical process explained in the previous chapter, for in both cases the goal is the same: the integration of the *animus* and *anima*, so that everything now to be developed is basically only the realization of spiritual alchemy by means of what could be called 'the alchemy of love'.

If, therefore—to resume our train of thought—the androgyne is the image of God in man, the complete union of the Lover and the Beloved will lead to Unity, that is to say to God. To begin with, *eros* is a dialectic of *me* and *you*, but when it develops in a truly and profoundly spiritual direction, the dialectic is resolved into an identification of me with you and you with me. Conjugal union becomes an awareness of Unity, it brings about a death of the egocentric self; you and I are unified and this unification provokes the awareness that there is none but *he*, or rather *He* or the *Self*, God. Marriage resolves duality, and consequently multiplicity, in the unity of Being. Jean Canteins magnificently developed this schema in the course of an article published in *Religion of the Heart* (1991), a collective work in homage to Frithjof Schuon. This unification is realized when one comes to see God in the other, when the face of the Beloved becomes the Face of God and at the same time the mirror reflecting that of the Lover. Ibn-Arabi again says,

> Man contemplates God in woman.... Contemplation of God in women is the most perfect, and the most intense union (in the sensible order) is the conjugal act.

In the same way the Persian mystic Ruzbehan Bagli, dear to Henri Corbin, develops the idea that lived human love is the necessary initiation to divine love: through the transfiguration of *eros* in each beloved, the unique Beloved is encountered, just as in each Divine Name the totality of Divine Names is to be found. The same doctrine exists in India where it is written, 'Truly, it is not for the love of the husband that the husband is dear, but for the love of Atma in him; truly it is not for the love of the wife that the wife is dear, but for the love of Atma in her' (*Brhadaranyaka Upanishad*, 2, 4, 5).

This metaphysics of love and marriage also forms the basis, under different modalities and in different language, of the Christian conception of marriage where its sacred character, in the highest sense, is there for us to see in its very qualification as a *sacrament*, a word which, in Christianity, is the equivalent of 'initiation', something that was clearly seen by Dionysios the Areopagite, as stated earlier. Similarly, St John Chrysostom did not hesitate to write, 'Thanks to love, man and woman steer towards life eternal and always attract further the grace of God . . . [marriage] is the sacrament of love' (*Hom.* 3 *in matrim*). For his part, Theophilus of Antioch said, 'God created Adam and Eve for the greatest love between them, *reflecting the mystery of Divine Unity*' (*Ad Autolyc.* 2, 28), which is what St Paul had already expressed in a formula that has not always been fully understood, 'Man . . . is the image and glory of God, and woman is the glory of man' (1 Cor. 11:7). In his beautiful essay *The Sacrament of Love*, Paul Evdokimov has shown in detail how Christian marriage is 'the unity of *two* persons in a *single* being': the persons are not suppressed, but their union makes of the dyad a monad, a third term that he qualifies as divine, in the image of what happens in the Trinity. And in connection with this he quotes these lines of the German Romantic F. von Baader, 'The goal of marriage is the reciprocal restoration of the heavenly or angelic image as it should be in man,' a text that accordingly refers us to the origins and missed destiny of Adam and Eve. In fact, the Christian conception of love and marriage is articulated by the stages of the 'story of salvation', leading humanity from Paradise to the Fall, from Fall to Redemption, and from Redemption to Glorification, which is altogether logical, given the role of first importance played by love in the common destiny of man and woman.

It is thus important to examine things in their origin, as related in the Genesis account of the creation of man. There we read that God created man in his image, male and female (1:26–27); this is the affirmation of the consubstantiality of the masculine and feminine principles forming the human monad Adam-Eve, the status of which is described in 2:6–25. The Fall (chap. 3) splits the monad into contrary masculinities and femininities, into pairs made of two polarized individualities, objectivized and situated externally to one another—but Christ, through His Grace, makes it possible to recover the initial unit in Himself, and this grace is what constitutes marriage as a 'sacrament'. The original order was reborn on the occasion of the 'Marriage at Cana', the account of which, read according to its inner meaning, tells of the restitution of the primordial state of the relationships between man and woman, Adam and Eve. And *it is here that we have the intervention of Mary*, whose role as the New Eve over against the New Adam is essential in order to bring about this restitution.

Let us re-examine these two phases of the story of the human couple so as to pinpoint all the implications in it.

Genesis offers two accounts of the creation of man, which has greatly embarrassed modern exegetes who, having lost the understanding of the Books of Moses according to traditional hermeneutics, have come up with nothing better than to imagine that we have here two accounts of the same facts, emanating from either different places or authors, badly stitched together, and, in short, juxtaposed. The first account is qualified as 'Elohist', and the second as 'Yahwist', and they are said to have issued from two 'schools of theology', the first, tending toward polytheism (because God is there called *Elohim*, which is a plural!), and the second monotheistic (because there the name *Yahweh* appears)—all of which is but a 'patchwork job' of positivist and rationalist criticism having no serious foundation. In reality, the two accounts do not say the same thing, at all; to be sure they recount the creation of man, but at two different stages, and even, to be more exact, three, which can be distinguished by referring to the hermeneutic of traditional Jewish commentators, and to that of Fabre d'Olivet—perhaps even more accurate, in a way, although it rejoins the former—which was completed by Chauvet, and which we have already mentioned.

In the first account, the man in question is not individual man; this primordial Adam is all of future humanity, as possibility, in the divine thought. And when it is said that in creating man, God created him male and female (*Zakar ou neqebah*), these words do not designate the human sexes, and even less individualities, but rather the double active-passive modality indispensable to a principial being who is to play a role in existential manifestation 'as the image', precisely, of God the Creator, in whom these two aspects are to be found on a higher level, as was seen in chapter 3.

In its commentary on this passage of Moses, the *Zohar* (I, 22A, B; II, 1586) says that the creation of primordial man, *Adam Qadmon*, in the divine 'image and likeness', is explained as follows: the 'image' denotes the active, male, spiritual Light of the Essence, of the 'Father', and the 'likeness', the light of the 'Mother', which is that of the 'darkness', darkness in a positive sense, to be sure, of feminine Receptivity, of virgin Substance (we have seen that this is the meaning of the *black color* of the statues of the Virgin that are under consideration). Put differently, God created man 'male', in the image of His Transcendence, His Light, His formative Act, and 'female' in the likeness of His Immanence, His Receptivity or generative Substance. This entire exegesis is quite thoroughly developed and explained in the great work of the late Leo Schaya, *La Creation en Dieu*. In any case, it was confirmed by Origen, who must have known it, seeing that he wrote, 'It is said that the spirit (of man) is male and that the soul can be called female' (*In Gen.* 4, 15).

In the second account in the Book of Moses, reference is made to the 'solitude' of Adam and to the creation of woman:

And the Lord God said, 'It is not good that the man should be alone; I will make him an help meet for him'; [and from a 'rib' taken from the man] the Lord God made a woman, and brought her unto the man. And Adam said, 'This is now bone of my bones, and flesh of my flesh: she shall be called Woman (*aishah*), because she was taken out of Man (*aish*). Therefore shall a man leave his father and his mother, and shall cleave unto his wife: and they shall be one flesh.' (Gen. 2:18–25)

The 'solitude' of Adam does not signify that he is deprived of woman in a concrete sense, but that he exists within the as yet 'unopened' unity of his nature and does not have at his disposal the faculties destined to put him in touch with the outer world. These faculties are within him in a latent state, and an act of the Creator is needed for them to be manifested so that Adam might accomplish his universal mission, namely to rule the entirety of living beings, and, first, as God's chosen mediator, to bestow on them the animating principle. God will thus give Adam a 'helper' (*ezer*), that is to say a faculty that will 'emerge' from his inmost recesses, which is expressed figuratively by the extraction of a rib. *Aishah*, the woman, then appears, that is to say, the auxiliary power enabling Adam to have contact with outwardness through the generation of the 'other' in the 'same', to use the language of Plato. *Aishah* represents an intermediary nature between pure spirituality and sensible effectuation; she is in touch with the sensible world and animality (without any pejorative sense); this is an affective and, to speak in the manner of the Scholastics, appetent faculty uniting the inner spiritual principle to outwardness. *Aishah* is the objectivation of the femininity of Adam, of his receptive substance. Again, Leo Schaya says, 'In her, Adam will be able to give himself to himself and himself receive himself and be *one* in the image of God.' This is what the rest of the sacred text expresses: Adam recognizes himself in *aishah* as 'she who is bone of my bones and flesh of my flesh' (that is to say essence of my essence and substance of my substance); this is why she shall be called 'woman' (*aishah*) because she has been taken from 'man' (*aish*); a lexical correlation that does not 'transfer' into English, Greek, or Latin.

We should note that at this point in this second chapter of the Book of Moses, corporeal or animal man, as he is at present, has not yet appeared. What we have here is an ontology of the Androgyne. Is this to say that at the stage of the terrestrial Paradise, woman, as a personal being, has not yet appeared? To ask this question is to raise an issue that has divided the exegetes. Some, like Origen, were tempted to think that Adam, before the Fall, was androgynous in the strict sense, that is to say not having at his side a woman outwardly objectified in an entirely separate being. Such a view, however, is improbable and accords badly with what is said in verse 25 of this chapter: 'The man shall leave his father and his mother and cleave unto his wife and they two shall become one flesh', the word 'flesh' having here the sense of 'living being', as is often the case in the Scriptures. According to the most orthodox interpretation, this text expresses the state of *two* distinct beings, so intimately united, however, that essentially they form but *one*. A final proof, it seems to us, against the first interpretation was given by Philip Sherrard in a study in the already cited collection, *Religion of the Heart*, where he says that the Virgin in heaven remains a woman and has not become some sort of bisexual being.

That said, we should remember that neither Adam nor his companion were corporal beings in the way of men and woman today.

They appeared as such only after the Fall and the expulsion from terrestrial Paradise; it was then, in fact, that God gave them a physical body as we know it, which *Genesis* calls 'coats of skin', and this is *when Adam called his Aishah Eve* (Gen. 3:20). What then was the state of Adam and his companion in the terrestrial Paradise? What emerges from the text of Genesis and the traditional commentaries, both those of the Jews and those of the Church Fathers, is that they had what is called an 'etheric body'. To recapitulate, these are the steps in the creation of man according to these commentaries: the uncreated state in God, his conception in the divine mind (*Adam Qadmon*); descent to the 'heavenly paradise', where his soul receives a subtle form; descent to the 'terrestrial paradise', where that form receives an etheric and incorruptible body; and, finally, the fall to the sensible world, where it is clothed in a new envelope, a perishable body that has emerged from the etheric substance of the edenic body. Let us specify, for those of our readers insufficiently informed concerning these matters, that the etheric body is so called because it is composed of 'ether' which, according to traditional cosmology, is the root-element of material bodies composed of the four elements, that is, the root-element and principle of these four elements that remains in a hidden state in coarse bodies. Ether itself is not material, but of the subtle order, and consequently is not subject to the limitations inherent in the state of beings and things belonging to the spatio-temporal world; in other words, the etheric body of man in Eden was similar to that of the resurrected Christ during the intermediate period between the Resurrection and Ascension. And, in connection with this, let us note that, like Christ, man in Eden had the ability to 'materialize' himself in a certain way so as to enter into contact with the sensible world over which he had been made regent, but he also had the ability to retire therefrom; it was precisely his decision not to withdraw from it, but rather to establish himself therein, that was the cause of his 'Fall'.

The question of man's progeny in Eden then presents itself as a corollary to the question just examined. Indeed, in the first account of the creation of man, God says, 'Be fruitful and multiply' (Gen. 1: 28). This divine command has always been interpreted to relate to the ends of marriage, namely the procreation of children. In the current state of humanity, these children are physical beings like their parents, but in the state of terrestrial Paradise, where man was clothed with an etheric and not a material body, it is certain that he was not able to give birth to children endowed with a physical body. Moreover, *Genesis* itself gives us the proof of this when it teaches that Adam and his wife only had carnal relations after their expulsion from earthly Paradise, that is to say, after receiving a material body, and that it was then that Eve gave birth to Cain and Abel (Gen. 4:1). We can therefore ask how man, in Eden, obeyed the precept 'Be fruitful and multiply.' If at that point they had progeny, which is likely, but of which we find no evidence in the biblical account, it would have been by way of 'relations' other than carnal, which is plainness itself, and of which the 'fruits' would have been descendents similar to their parents. Revelation has not enlightened us concerning this matter.

If we have lingered somewhat over these matters, this is because, as will be seen, they have a bearing upon the modalities of marriage as conceived in the Christian perspective, and, consequently, on the role Mary is called to play therein—this being our principle problem, which, despite appearances, has not been lost to view.

What characterizes the situation of the human couple after the Fall is the separation into opposing *sexes*; the word itself, moreover, clearly says as much: *sexus*, in Latin, comes from the root meaning 'to cut' (verb *secare*). Separation leads to rivalry and opposition, which is noticeable from the start, for after the 'fault' Adam put the responsibility on Eve, and the original harmonious union is from that point destroyed, simultaneously with the degradation of the 'flesh'. Through His redemptive act, however, Christ has restored it, at least in principle, for the Edenic state is not *effectively* re-established for the *whole* of humanity, and will not be until after the Judgment; but is re-established in a *virtual*, but nevertheless very real fashion through baptism, which makes it possible for the individual, starting now, to regain by means of Grace a state substantially similar to the primordial state in expectation of the final and total reintegration. This applies particularly to the relationship between the sexes and to marriage. Christ has destroyed the curse weighing upon the 'flesh', reconciling the latter with the spirit and enabling man and woman to recover the harmony existing before the Fall.

What could be called the 'charter' of Christian marriage, constituting its 'heart' and making of it a sacrament, that is to say an initiation in the highest possible sense, is spelled out in the celebrated passage of the *Epistle to the Ephesians* already quoted, where the Apostle clearly gives the teaching of Jesus.

> The husband [he writes] is the head of the wife, even as Christ is the head of the Church, which is His body.... Husbands, love your wives, even as Christ also loved the Church.... So ought men to love their wives as their own bodies... For this cause shall a man leave his father and his mother, and shall be joined unto his wife, and they two shall be one flesh. This is a great mystery: but I speak concerning Christ and the Church' (Eph. 5:22–32).

This language may appear somewhat enigmatic and is only understandable when put in the context of a thoroughly Jewish way of envisaging the relationship of man to God. Along with the gifts that will reach their fullness at the coming of the Messiah, God was considered 'married' to the 'Community of Israel'. And, effectively, Jesus is himself identified with the 'Husband'—directly in the Gospels of Matthew (9:15) and Mark (2:19–20), and indirectly in the parable of the Ten Virgins (Matt 25:1–13). St John the Baptist also speaks of him in this way:

> He who possesses the Wife is the Husband; but the beloved of the Husband, who is present and awaits him, is ravished with joy on account of the voice of the Husband; this joy, which is mine, has been accomplished.

The language is directly in line with the whole Hebrew tradition. This manner of speaking of Christ supposes Him to be considered as the heavenly Husband of the Community of Israel, a community destined to be enlarged to that of His Church. This Hebraic tradition is rooted and expressed in a particular way in the *Song of Songs*, that nuptial song celebrating under a symbolic form the marriage of God with His People. In his commentary on the famous *Song*, based entirely upon Jewish exegeses, Paul Vulliaud recalls that the two protagonists of the sacred nuptial poem represent the 'King' and the 'Queen', whom we have already met before. The 'King', son of *Hokmah* and *Binah*, 'Wisdom' and 'Intelligence', is *Tiphereth*, that is to say *Adam Qadmon*, celestial Adam, the archetype of earthly Adam; the 'Queen', is *Malkuth*, a term meaning literally 'Kingdom' and in certain respects assimilated to the Shekhina, 'The Spouse of the Holy One, blessed be He!'; and it is equally the Community of Israel. P. Vulliaud has no difficulty in showing that it is this doctrine that underlies and permits an explanation of the elliptic and, at first sight, somewhat incomprehensible language of St Paul, which we read above and which is plainly that of Christ. It is clear that in St Paul's text, Christ is *Tiphereth*, the head of the Community of Israel, that the Shekhina is the 'Body' of Tiphereth, according to an alto-gether traditional acceptation, and that, for St Paul, earthly mar-riage ought to be an image of the celestial marriage of the 'King' and 'Queen.' Besides, does he not say elsewhere, when speaking to the Christians of the 'community' of the 'church' of Corinth, 'I have betrothed you and presented you as a pure virgin to a unique Hus-band' (1 Cor. 11:2)? In St Paul's teaching on marriage, Adam and Eve represent Tiphereth and Malkuth or the Shekhina; Adam and Eve will be *two* persons in a *single* 'Body'; Tiphereth and Malkuth will become individuals in the original mystery of the creation of man, which is what sexual duality symbolizes. But Malkuth is reunited with Tiphereth so as to raise up the present world, sanctify it through good works, and reintroduce it to the 'plenitude of the glory'. Now herein, also, lies the mystery of marriage. The *Zohar*, quoted by P. Vulliaud, says that man is not truly man unless he real-izes here below that state of original man, that is to say the *holy* union of man and woman. St Paul also writes: 'Neither is the man without the woman, neither the woman without the man, in the Lord' (1 Cor. 11:11). And for the Kabbalists, as we have seen, every conjugal union is the union of Tiphereth and Malkuth.

Thus marriage, according to Christ, has initiatic value as sacra-ment, allowing baptismal initiation, which is virtual reintegration into the primordial state before the Fall, to be effective. *Eros*, within the perspective of Christic Grace, makes the realization of the inti-mate union of man and woman possible, union that signs and seals the image of God in the human being; which leads us back to the concept of the primordial androgyne.

Speaking of man and woman, Jesus says, 'They two shall be one flesh. Wherefore they are no more *two*, but *one* flesh; what therefore God has *joined* together, let no man *put asunder*' (Matt 19:4–6). Paul Evdokimov quite rightly says that if these words of Christ proclaim the indissolubility of marriage, which they certainly do, their primary aim is to reconstitute the androgynous state, the state wherein man and woman are not 'separated'; moreover, it is this original model that alone justifies the indissolubility of marriage. Jesus is saying, in effect, that having re-established the primordial state of *union*, He commands us not to repeat the experience of the Fall by transforming it into a state of 'separation'. That Jesus had the androgynous state in mind here is proved by a 'saying' addressed to his disciples reported in the *Gospel of Thomas* (not Gnostic):

> When you make the *two one* . . . and if you make the masculine and feminine into one, so that the masculine no longer be masculine and the feminine feminine, then you will enter the Kingdom.

This saying is also reported in the *Gospel of the Egyptians* quoted by St Clement of Alexandria in his third *Stromata*. It is obvious that this text is not to be interpreted as proclaiming a suppression of the masculine and feminine—which would be absurd, since it is their complementarity that is 'divine image'—but their fusion without confusion in a single being, 'a single body', in which they are not abolished but, on the contrary, completed in unity. It is in this spirit that another assertion of Christ that 'in heaven there will be no more marriage and the elect will be like angels', should be understood; Christ does not mean the elect will be asexual, an hypothesis refuted, as we have said, by the celestial state of the Virgin. He means simply that with glorified bodies there will no longer be 'carnal union'. When we speak of the androgyne in connection with man before the Fall and of the Christic doctrine of the marriage of 'two in one flesh', we must understand by this an 'androgynous dyad'—again P. Evdokimov's expression—which transcends the duality of the sexes through integration, and not suppression, and rejoins the state of man and woman before the Fall.

In order to grasp the full importance of Christ's doctrine on marriage, it is necessary to see all that is contained in the parallel drawn by St Paul between the relationship of Christ to the Church and man to woman. The Church is the Wife of the Husband, Christ; this Wife is called by St Paul 'The Body of Christ'. Moreover, by asserting that the woman is the 'body' of the man, the Apostle invites us to establish a connection between *woman* and *Church*. This means that the intimate, spousal union of Christ with the Church, which is His 'Body', is reflected in the intimate union of a man and the woman who is his 'body', in conformity with the words of Adam, 'This is bone of my bones, flesh of my flesh.' And this makes it an intimate union established and sealed through the Grace of the Holy Spirit poured out on this 'domestic church' that is marriage, a church instituted by the sacrament, the goal of which is intimate union in one body, in the image of the total Church, in which every couple will finally be united to Christ.

By this we see to what spiritual level sanctified marriage is raised—to such a point, in fact, that the flesh, which on account of sin was first considered to be vile, is redeemed, and participates in the sacred. It needs to be clearly understood, in fact, that if the flesh was cursed after the Fall, 'it was only,' as Frithjof Schuon says,

> according to the relationship of existential discontinuity... between the phenomenon and the archetype ... but not according to that of essential continuity. In one sense the flesh is separated from the spirit, but in another it is united to it in manifesting it, and prolongs it *to the extent that it is recognized as situated on the unitive vertical, and not on the separative horizontal.*

The latter case is that of the Adamic 'error'; the other, that of the sacrament that restores the flesh to its essential relationship to the spirit.

We should also not be surprised to read the following lines given by a monk in his account of the Life of St Ida of Herzfeld, wife of the Comte Egbert (tenth century), that Dom J. Leclerq quotes in his book *Le mariage vu par les moines au XII siecle*:

The moment they are two in a single body, there is in them one and the same operation of the Holy Spirit: while they are entwined through the ties of their outer, that is to say, sensible union, this indivisible action of the Holy Spirit enflames them with a greater inner love with regard to heavenly realities.

We can see that here we are far from the pessimistic Puritanism alluded to at the beginning of the chapter. What is more, the doctrine so clearly expressed in the text just read is perfectly orthodox. It is the same that St Bernard, for example, develops in his sermons on the *Song of Songs*, where he shows that the 'carnal union' of the spouses (*carnale connubium*) is parallel to the 'spiritual marriage' (*spirituale matrimonium*) that unites the soul to God. Put differently, this is the traditional Hebraic doctrine according to which, when the spouses are chastely united, the Shekhina is in the midst of them. In short, what is produced as a result of sacramental grace is exactly a transformation which, according to the alchemical formula, consists of 'embodying the spirit and spiritualizing the body,' which is an aspect of the realization of the androgynous state that is the goal of Christian marriage.

How is this goal to be attained? According to Philip Sherrard, whom we have already cited, man and woman realize it, or at least tend thereto, by living as if in the earthly Paradise—which was not a 'place', as too many people believe, but a 'state' of being—by living according to the rule of Paradise before the Fall, that is to say by living a *life of relationship*, a relationship of love, of love considered as a quality of living. This involves 'loving one another in God', which means that to love the Other is to see God in him. The husband loves in his wife the mystery she reveals, and vice-versa. In such love, it is God who arouses the eros of the lovers, love without egoism, that does not desire to 'possess' the Other, but to be 'reborn in them' and transfigured through them. Each activates the aspiration of the other to grow so as to progress to the perfection that is the purpose of their earthly existence. This is done through each regarding the other as a manifestation of divine Love. The result is a reciprocal spiritualization of their being, a going beyond the sensible state towards the spiritual, and the contemplation of God in each other.

This is the relationship we have spoken of that makes possible the realization of the perfection of the spouses, because each possesses specific qualities corresponding to the divine qualities alluded to earlier; for example, woman sees strength in man while he sees beauty, etc. in her. Through this exchange of qualities they are mutually enriched and fulfilled, and rise again to the original state.

Now, in this process towards reintegration, the role of woman is primordial. She helps man to understand himself, to realize his being, to 'become what he is'. Woman's charism, says P. Evdokimov, is 'to give birth to the man hidden in the heart.' And, also in this connection, we can say that woman is always 'mother', that maternity envisaged in its widest sense, is her fundamental characteristic. This maternal role is rooted in the Divine Maternity; if God is masculine in His Transcendence, He is feminine in His Infinity, Beauty, Goodness and Self-diffusion. In many places in his work, Frithjof Schuon has developed this idea that 'Woman, in Her highest aspect, is united to this Infinity and enables the Source to be everywhere: she is the cause of Creation and consequently the means of re-ascending to the Source.' She makes it possible for beings to participate in Divinity and exercises a liberating function; to return to alchemical terminology, faced with masculine reason and strength, woman exerts a 'liquefying' power over a certain 'hardness' characterizing man, enabling him to come out of himself, to 'melt his ego' and lift his spirit from earth to Heaven.

Concerning this, it is enlightening to note that in all the great literary works treating of spiritualized love, the path of celestial *eros* is taught by a woman: Diotima in Plato's *Symposium*, Beatrice with Dante, who called her 'the beautiful Lady who raises to Heaven' (*Paradiso* x, 91), or again, the unknown one whom J. Du Bellay celebrates in evoking the celestial abode:

> *There, oh my soul, to the highest heaven led,*
> *You will come to know the Idea hid,*
> *Of the beauty that here I adore.*

And Goethe, at the end of his *Faust*, wrote the famous words:

> *The Eternal Feminine draws us Heavenwards.*

Now, the Eternal Feminine is manifested in the world, and has a name: it is the Virgin Mary, whom we thus rediscover at the end of this chapter, after a digression on marriage that may have appeared long and perhaps extraneous to our subject, whereas in fact it is profoundly implicated, for the Marian Mystery is the mystery of woman, mother, and wife, the mystery at the heart of man's destiny. All we have said above about the role of woman obviously applies, and eminently so, to Mary, who, as the Christian form of the *Magna Mater*, reveals in her earthly and heavenly manifestation the supreme archetype of the Eternal Feminine, celestial Wisdom, the divine Shakti, and *Maya*, as was shown at length in Chapter 3.

But *Maya* presents a certain ambiguity as a result of its double ascending and descending movement, which, as we have said, is that of Creation; thus there is a *descending* and an *ascending Maya*. In its descent, *Maya* manifests a world of appearances that can either enlighten or deceive man, whereas in its ascent it is capable of revealing God to man and of leading to Him. And the same applies to woman, who, as Frithjof Schuon has clearly shown, in a certain respect appears as that which exteriorizes and enthralls, because feminine psychology, on a purely natural level and outside of a spiritual valorization, admits of a tendency towards the concrete, the existential, the subjective, and sentimental. This was Eve's sin, which consisted in dragging Adam into the adventure towards outwardness and the sensible. But woman, as *Maya*, also has the opposite capacity: the beauty of woman can and should reveal to man the Beauty and beatitude of the Divine Essence.

Such is *Mary's* function, the opposite of *Eve's*. The secret of 'salvation through woman' lies in the double nature of *Maya*, which can attract towards the outer, the world, the sensible, etc. but also towards the inner, the spirit, the heart, the Divine. *Eve* is 'life'—which is precisely what her name signifies—'life' separated from the 'spirit'; she is descending *Maya*. *Mary* is 'Grace', ascending and reintegrating *Maya*, personification of the Shekhina, of Holy Wisdom, the maternal and virginal feminine presence of God in the world. According to P. Evdokimov, *the vocation of Mary and of every woman in imitation of her, is, 'as mother, to protect the world of mankind, and, as Virgin, to purify it by giving it a soul.'*

Mary protects mankind by obstructing Satan in order to counter-act Eve's action in Paradise. 'Woman, behold thy son,' said the dying Christ, indicating John and, through him, all of humanity. This utterance of Christ introduces Mary as the 'New Eve' at the same time as 'Mother of men'. Opposing the seductions of the 'world', she is the 'Most Pure Virgin', the 'Most Chaste Virgin', as her Litanies call her, and, above all, the 'Mother of Beautiful Love', the manifestation of that 'Celestial Virgin Sophia', of whom J. Boehme spoke, to whom Adam and Eve, before the Fall, were 'united in a sacred and hidden marriage.' This Virgin, he says further, 'had taken flight', but with Mary she is once again among men. In his *Theosophia practica*, Gichtel says it is she who inspires man to seek her in *eros* and woman, by surmounting excessive carnal desire after the likeness of Mary, in whom the rebirth of the soul is accomplished.

Let it be clearly understood: the purity and chastity inspired by this sort of 'imitation of Mary' are not a denial of sexuality, but rather are bound up with it. *Eros*, pushed to its noble limit in mar-riage, is transcended in something that surpasses it, since the indi-vidual self is itself surpassed. The energy of eros, controlled and mastered by chastity, becomes more powerful, completely clarifying and transforming itself to the extent that the mind is fixed upon something transcendent; its force changes direction and it 'flows upwards.' Chastity is dependent upon that quality known in Greek as *sophrosyne* or 'moderation', a spiritual quality that is the power of integrity, integrity of the feelings, the soul. With regard to this, P. Evdokimov shows that sexuality is surpassed through its own sym-bolism; as a symbol of Unity, with reference to the principial andro-gyne, it is detached from pure animality, is transcended as it approaches the spiritual integrity of the single being and, in this way, confers an 'ascending dynamism' on man.

When this development of eros is sufficiently advanced, the latter is purified of all lust, and the gaze contemplates divine Beauty behind sensual appearances. Thus Ramakrishna said to his wife, 'I see in you an incarnation of the Divine Mother (Durga) who tri-umphs over the demon of lust,' and, further, 'I look upon every woman as my Divine Mother.' In *The Ladder*, St John Climacus mentions altogether similar conduct on the part of Bishop Nonnus of Edessa. Finding himself in the presence of the beautiful dancer Pelagia, who was nude, Nonnus

> through his praises made of it an occasion to adore and glorify the sovereign Beauty, of whom this woman was only the handi-work, and he felt himself completely transported by the fire of divine love, dissolving into tears of joy.

Such a man has already attained the heavenly state; according to John Climacus 'he is raised incorruptible even before the universal resurrection.'

To aspire, if not to attain such a degree of purity, at least to approach it as closely as possible, the merciful aid of the Virgin, *Virgo purissima* and *immaculata*, is needed. And in the familiar scene of the 'Marriage at Cana' (John 2:1–12), the Gospel of St John contains a passage that sheds abundant light upon this aspect of Mary's role in the spiritual life of the couple.

A somewhat superficial reading of this account might leave the impression that the occasion of the marriage itself was only the pre-text and the setting intended to highlight the miracle that inaugu-rated Jesus' public life. In reality, though, the opposite is true; the marriage is at the forefront, and the miracle serves it directly. Two conclusions should be drawn from this: first, the importance of marriage in the mind of Jesus, who honors the ceremony with his presence, and, second, the importance of Mary's role on this occa-sion, an importance inversely proportional to the modesty accom-panying her intervention with her Son.

What is more, the story of Cana should once again be situated within the series of Gospel passages in which Christ symbolically refers to marriage and marriage festivities to describe the life of the elect in His Kingdom, an attitude that reconfirms his high estima-tion of marriage—which is why the patristic tradition rightly saw the feast at Cana as a figure of the Kingdom.

It is also appropriate to consider the two levels on which the event unfolds, the plane of earthly marriage and the plane of the mystery of redemption, and, above all—for this is what presently interests us—their co-penetration, in that the destiny of the human couple is included in the plan of redemption considered as a marriage, in which Jesus becomes the spouse of human nature in order to unite it to divine nature.

Now, this spiritual marriage is symbolized by what is at the heart of the miracle at Cana: the 'mystery of the water and the wine'. The symbolism is so fundamental that the Church, referring to Jesus' miracle, recalls it in its eucharistic liturgy, for at the moment of the Offertory in the Latin rite, the priest mixes water with the wine of the sacrifice while praying,

> Oh God, who created human nature in a marvelous manner and, in a more marvelous manner still, re-established it in its first dignity, grant us, through *the mystery of this water and this wine*, to participate in the divinity of Him who deigned to be united to our humanity, Our Lord Jesus Christ.

The 'mystery of the water and the wine' is therefore the mystery of the reintegration of human nature (the water) into the spiritual life (the wine), or, more precisely, the transformation of the water into wine, that is to say divinization. In the Judeo-Christian tradition wine is in fact the symbol of the higher, spiritual life. Besides, there is a sequel to the miracle at Cana: the Lord's Supper of Maundy Thursday, where, through a new transformation, the wine becomes the saving and vivifying *Blood*.

This reminder allows us to evaluate the meaning of the miracle at Cana correctly with regard to the destiny of the couple and of marriage. The Virgin Mary says to Jesus, 'They have no more wine.' Over and above the immediate sense, which concerns the unfolding of the meal, these words must be understood in a much higher sense, as is often the case in the Gospels, especially that of St John, which sense, however, is always related to the event. 'They have no more wine', that is to say the wine of the spirit has deserted mankind, and nominally, in the present case, the man and woman who are to be married; the chastity, purity, and integrity of their being have disappeared, having fallen back into the impasse of the separated, nay opposed, sexes, into the state of fallen nature that is prey to the passions represented by the 'water' in the urns. Christ changes this water into wine, thereby giving back to man and woman the life of the spirit and transforming the passions into new love, a love in which restored purity and chastity transform sexuality and re-establish the spiritual integrity of the being.

Now—and this is the essential point for our purpose—*all this happens at the instigation of Mary*; it is she, acting in her capacity as intercessor, in her capacity as *mediatrix*, whom the Church has officially declared 'Mediatrix of all Graces', who convinces Christ to perform the miracle of transformation. Also, on this occasion, we cannot avoid referring to all that was said in the previous chapter concerning the 'alchemical function' of the Virgin.

Thus, within the framework and under the guise of a wedding celebrated in a small town of Galilee, what St John has in reality related to us is nothing less than Jesus' institution of marriage as a sacrament. The intimate structure of the scene at Cana, which, although hidden, appears luminous to an attentive reader, consists in a parallel between two 'couples', the groom and his bride, and Jesus and Mary, the former being of Adam and Eve and the latter of the New Adam and the New Eve. With regard to this, it is worth paying attention to how Jesus addresses Mary; He calls her 'Woman', and does the same at Calvary, when, pointing to St John, He says to her: 'Woman behold thy Son'. The word 'woman' in this context is pregnant with meaning, and is given its fullest significance; Jesus is designating Mary as *the* Woman, the earthly manifestation of the Eternal Feminine. On both occasions, Christ's words introduce Mary as the New Eve: at Calvary, as 'Mother', 'Mother of the Living' and Mother of mankind, represented by John, and at Cana, as 'Woman' and 'Wife', the archetypal model of the wife for men. And she can effectively be the model of wives, since she is the 'Spouse of God', 'Spouse of Christ', as we saw when, following Fr Bulgakov, we showed that the Theanthropy or Divine-humanity of Christ, which is intended to be that of mankind, is constitutionally androgynous in its essence, and that, in its earthly manifestation, it appeared in the *two* persons of Jesus *and* Mary, who restored the primordial pre-Fall androgyne. Now, marriage, raised to the level of sacrament by Jesus, *mysteriously identifies the spouses with Christ and Mary*, as the liturgy itself shows, at least in the Byzantine rite, where the future spouses are placed before the iconostasis, the groom facing the icon of Christ and the bride the icon of the Virgin. This liturgical practice is like a translation into gesture of the words of St Paul comparing a man's relationship to his wife with that of Christ to the Church, which is the 'Body of Christ', but to which Mary is also assimilated through her official title of 'Mother of the Church'. From this it can be clearly seen how, thanks to the sacrament, 'marriage is a mysterious icon of the Church,' as St John Chrysostom writes, and how it brings the spouses into the latter, fitting them into the Body of the Church that is the Body of Christ. We are in the presence of a series of symbolic 'binomials': Man-Woman, Husband-Wife, Christ-Church, Christ-Virgin, Christ-Mystical Body, Church-Mystical Body of Christ, Wife-Body of Husband, which, in the language of algebra, can be 'reduced' to each other, thus revealing the analogical correspondences uniting them. To return to our subject, we see in particular that the relationship of Christ to the Virgin, which is that of Husband to Wife, is analogous to that of Christ to the Church, which is his Body, as, according to St Paul, the wife is the 'body of the husband'. Now, this idea of the 'body' leads us to the idea of Creation, which is considered as the 'Body of God', and which is contained in the 'Mystical Body of Christ', therefore in the Church, which, in its total extension, is Creation restored and therefore incarnated in the Virgin, who is 'Mother of the Church'. And the charism of the Virgin Mary is to help man to fit into the Mystical Body, causing him to become aware of his limited self and of the membership of his personality, linked to all the others in the universal chorus of Wisdom, Sancta Sophia, who is Mary; or again, Universal Nature, *Prakriti*, 'Body of God', *Purusha*—and by this we are raised even to the supreme Reality in its two aspects, the Absolute and the Infinite, reflected in the created as the Masculine and the Feminine.

Two conclusions can be drawn from this: first, that the union of man and woman, when restored to its original integrity, provides the most common spiritual way of re-ascending to God; and then, that it is the role of woman, in that she is especially related to Nature, to draw man into this spiritual ascent, and that consequently this is eminently the role of Mary, who, for the man, should represent the 'Heavenly Lady', with whom he will identify his spouse, and who is, for the spouse, the inspiring model of her behavior.

Having reached the end of our book, we seem to have momentarily forgotten the Black Virgin. In reality, however, she has never left us, for basically it is she who has made it possible for us to penetrate to the heart of the Marian Mystery and thereby the mystery of the depths of Being. In the grottoes of Rocamadour and Lourdes, in the crypts of Chartres and Marseilles, she continues to play for Christians the role previously played by the neolithic Great Mother in her successive hypostases: she was, and remains, essentially the *initiatic mother,* she who traverses death for us in order to transcend it and introduce us to the understanding of mysteries, the mystery of the world, of creation, the mystery of Nature, of life, of man and woman, the supreme mystery of the depths of God in the Infinitude of the Godhead from which she and everything else arose; finally, it is she who, through the will of Christ, gives birth to man as son of God.

In promoting as it has the cult of the Mother of God, according it its full compass, we see that Christianity, faithful to its character of being a 'universal' religion, has succeeded in integrating in a form compatible with Semitic monotheism an essential element of the *religio perennis,* the Eternal Feminine, an awareness of which is always more or less obscurely present in the human soul, and which needs to be objectified in order to ensure the latter's spiritual equilibrium.

Printed in Great Britain
by Amazon

43777235R00111